AN AGENDA FO[...]

Frank Field was elected as Member of Parliament for Birkenhead in 1979. He has been a front-bench spokesperson on education and social security, and was the director of the Child Poverty Action Group. He is Chairman of the Social Security Select Committee.

FRANK FIELD

An Agenda for Britain

HarperCollins*Publishers*

HarperCollins*Publishers*
77–85 Fulham Palace Road,
Hammersmith, London W6 8JB

A Paperback Original 1993
1 3 5 7 9 8 6 4 2

A catalogue record for this book
is available from the British Library

ISBN 0 00 638226 6

Set in Sabon

Printed in Great Britain by
HarperCollinsManufacturing Glasgow

For Nick and Cathy Warren

CONTENTS

PREFACE

While I have added a substantial amount of new material, this book began life as the University of Durham's Bernard Gilpin's Pastoral Lectures for 1993. My first thanks goes to the Department of Theology who invited me to Durham. The magnificence of that city was matched by spring weather and the hospitality of Sheridan Gilley, the Chairman of the department, Meg Gilley and Sheridan's colleagues.

A second wave of thanks goes to four people. Jill Hendey worked on the manuscript in addition to all her other work. Matthew Owen did likewise, as well as trace material and discuss with me the book's line of argument. I am particularly grateful to them for absorbing the considerable amount of extra work that producing a book entails, and doing so in such a way as to make working with them such a pleasure. Damian Leeson went through the whole document and sharpened both the prose and presentation. In Rebecca Wilson I was the beneficiary of being given by HarperCollins an editor whose talents were matched by a dedication to a production of books of the highest technical quality.

John Grigg, Lord Bonham Carter and Calum MacDonald read through the first draft of the introduction. I am grateful to them for their comments. In addition, Mark Bonham Carter read through the original lectures, commented upon and encouraged me to publish them. He also kindly thought of the book's title. Robert Twigger, Robert Clements, Richard Cracknell, Adrian Crompton, Richard Dewdney, Nicola Chedgey, Ed MacGregory, Mahmed Nawaz and Jane Dyson of the House of Commons Library produced a number of statistical papers, and Dora Clark and Andrew Parker traced innumerable sources for me. MPs are blessed by having a library research staff whose qualities are unsurpassed. While I am grateful to all these people who helped produce this volume, its opinions are my responsibility, as are any errors which have escaped their watchful eyes.

The book is dedicated to Nick and Cathy Warren. Nick worked with me as solicitor to the Birkenhead Resource Unit and Cathy too worked for the Unit in a voluntary capacity. During Nick's twelve year's stewardship my constituents received a Rolls-Royce legal service. His standing in the town is testament to that, as was my vote at general elections. Due largely to the happy fallout from Nick's work, of which I was the beneficiary, Birkenhead was turned into one of the safest seats in the country. The book's dedication is, therefore, a small but public means of thanking Nick and Cathy for the care they lavished on so large a number of my poorer constituents.

FRANK FIELD
June 1993

AN AGENDA FOR BRITAIN

The Vision Thing

Poor old George Bush got it right. Stumbling through the presidential election campaign he realized what was missing. In true Bush style he blurted out that he was short on 'the vision thing'. What was true of the defeated Republican campaign is also true for a defeated Labour Party.

The 'vision thing' affects both Government and Opposition parties. That the Government is almost bankrupt of ideas is not surprising. Four election wins in a row and fourteen years in office is enough to convince any group of human beings that they are destined to remain there to the end of their days. Winning, after all, is the major test, so why worry too much if Cabinet Ministers cannot spell out in precise terms what the Government is trying to achieve? And yet?

In times past the pendulum has always swung back. So why won't it next time? That must be the worry at the back of the mind of every Government supporter. It is, however, far from the back of the mind of Labour activists. In order to talk up morale a political law of averages reigns in Labour Party thinking. No swing back on the last three occasions makes it more, not less, certain that the swing will occur next time. It is a belief of all gamblers that their chances improve the more they lose. This is not the case, neither in the casino nor in the election arena. Political memories are inevitably short. No member of the current House of Commons was elected to the 1945 Parliament, so that the pendulum years appear to most politicians as the natural rhythm of politics. But such a pattern does not fit the decades before 1945 when the Conservatives were rarely out of power. The dreadful thought which ought to be stalking the Left is that the close fought elections of the early

13

1950s and mid-1970s might prove to be the exceptions rather than the rule.

Fundamental changes have been taking place which make a regular sharing of power between the two main parties a less, rather than more, likely future turn of events. For one thing, the swings which do occur, and which would have swept the board for the Opposition party, now merely reduce the overall size of the Government's majority in the House of Commons. The 2 per cent swing gained last time by Neil Kinnock would have been enough to land him in Downing Street if only the election had been held in the 1950s rather than in the 1990s. It is the size of the Government's lead amongst voters on election day, combined with the disappearance of the traditional marginal seat, which is part of the stumbling block. The clear polarization into ever more safe seats presents a microcosm of what is happening across the country.

The nagging doubt of many Labour activists is that the change in British politics is more fundamental than this. Two forces are at work. The first is that the social groups from which Labour's traditional support has come have shrunk, are shrinking and look set to shrink further. It is as though Labour is trying to advance on a downward moving escalator.

But why is Labour on a down escalator in the first place? Here lies the second and more deadly of the two forces working against the Party. A large number of people raised in Labour-voting homes have simply walked away from the Party. In fairness many of these people would argue that Labour has simultaneously been marching off in a different direction anyway. These voters compare their past loyalty to Labour to the bonds which they used to have with their school friends. At the time, few people could be more important. However, even in the most stable of circumstances people can grow apart. Britain, far from being stable, has seen not merely the collapse of its traditional manufacturing base but of new strains throughout its social fabric. Partly as a result of this, but also because of rising living standards, people are on the move. A third of all households moved during the last decade. Old ties and friendships are thus broken, commitments reduced to memories which are valuable as part of our past, but definitely no longer of present significance. As with the ties of friendship, so too with political parties.

It is as though the country has been shaken up in a gigantic political kaleidoscope. Many of us, with different aspirations, have settled down in different places and are relating to different areas and people. Class loyalties have been loosened and in many instances have simply disintegrated. The political kaleidoscope might well be shaken again; the Government could simply fall apart. Whilst it came close to doing so in the twelve months after winning the 1992 election, the Opposition cannot rely upon it doing so again. The Government may lack vision but it enjoys exercising power which it will not give up easily. The Government may be divided over Europe, but John Major is no Peel. His indentureship in Mrs Thatcher's Whips Office should not be forgotten: if his apprenticeship there taught him anything it was how to hold a party together in the roughest of political hurricanes.

The shaking of the political kaleidoscope has changed many people's perspective of the Labour Party. This is not simply because voters remember the rule of the bullies in the early 1980s. It is one thing to have one's life run by a series of barely competent Governments. Incompetence is a widely shared human failing, we are all incompetent in different ways. It is quite a different ball game to think of electing a party that has cowered before political extremism in its own ranks. Those images of supposed Labour Party supporters ranting and screaming at Labour leaders have become too much part of the folk memory of all too many voters for an easy accord to be again struck between the ruled and those wishing to rule. And there are still examples – though fewer, thank goodness – of this behaviour at a local government level. But each time there is an exposure of such an instance the scar tissue which the national party has been so carefully growing is ripped off.

The importance of such memories in deciding how to vote are underplayed by the Party élite, many of whom have little day-to-day contact with voters. For example, most do not ride on buses, their main means of transport being their own private car. The private car, and the need for security, has had a profound impact on the direct link between senior politicians and voters. Some of my constituents remember seeing photographs of Ramsay MacDonald and Stanley Baldwin hailing cabs at the corner of Downing Street and Whitehall. After some Cabinet meetings Attlee would adjourn to a bar on Liverpool Street Station. He would be accompanied there only by his Parliamentary Private Secretary (Roy Jenkins's father) and they would travel by a Circle line underground train. Such mixing is impossible now and without it senior politicians are dangerously exposed to hearing only what they want to hear.

The Party's negative image has been compounded by our painfully slow adjustment to Mrs Thatcher's violent shake-up of the political kaleidoscope. Indeed in some areas the adjustment has still to take place. Many of her changes were to the public's liking and good. For example, bringing the trade unions within the law, rather than setting a law by which the trade unions agreed to be bound. This Barbara Castle tried to implement and it should have been a Labour reform. Likewise, giving members control over their union ought to have been a Labour reform. However, far from being advocated by Labour, both reforms were bitterly opposed by the Party, and some members have still to accept the new accord. It is no use Labour's breast swelling with pride now as it claims to be the party fighting vested interests here, there, and everywhere except in respect to the block vote's operation in Labour Party affairs. Such posturing does not present the image of a party ready for government.

The list could be extended. But the message is clear. Not once since 1979 did Labour break free, leapfrog the Thatcher Government and start setting out its own stall with wares relevant to the new world. Changes were made but only after one, or sometimes two, election defeats. Had the Party embraced the 'one person—one vote' principle when it was first proposed this would have been part of Labour's new stance, rather than a reform seen to be emanating from the SDP. Selling council houses similarly could have been to the Party's advantage. In Labour's hands the resources raised would have been used to replenish stock and prevent the rise of the sink estates which now pockmark so much of the country.

But, some will say, look at the opinion polls. Yet in past parliaments the polls predicted future Labour success. Now, with Labour's enormous lead, the length of time the Conservative Government has been in office, its ability to make a mess of things, all point to a Labour success next time. This is as comfortable a reading of events as it is a misleading one.

However, in a country which appears to many voters to be a one-party state, by-elections and opinion polls have assumed a new role: they have partially replaced the Opposition's function of harassing the Government. Most Government seats are now unsafe in a by-election. Whilst the electorate enjoys turning out a member of the ruling party at a by-election to express its anger at the latest piece of Government nonsense, this form of protest is limited and, above all, safe, as was evident at the last general election where every seat lost by the Government in the previous Parliament was won back handsomely.

Opinion polls, which now play a crucial part in our democratic process, serve a similar role of giving the Government a rough time. Voters trying to get government policy modified or changed willingly mislead the pollsters. The trouble is that politicians have yet to wake up to what is going on. The polls give voters a chance to double- and sometimes treble-bluff the Government. Clearly, the more they are used in this way the less accurate they are as a guide to how voters might behave two or three years hence at a general election. It would be foolish therefore for Labour, or any party, to read the polls as we might have done in the 1950s or 1960s.

The polls, then, give no accurate guide to what voters will actually do on polling day. Moreover, the long-term socio-economic trends are against the Party. So what actions should

Labour take? Given the seriousness of the situation I believe it imperative for the Party to develop a two-track strategy. The first is to go for an all-out win next time. The second is simultaneously to plan sharing power with the Liberal-Democrats as a serious fall-back position. A contradictory approach? When asked about holding what might be contradictory positions, Jimmy Thomas, a Minister in Ramsay MacDonald's Labour Government replied that, if you couldn't ride two horses at once there was no point being part of the circus. And while it is a mistake to think of political life only in terms of the circus there are common elements to both activities.

In planning for an outright win Labour must ask itself the most fundamental question of all: what is it that Labour believes it can and should add to political life that no other party does or can contribute? Once the question of what Labour believes in is asked we are immediately faced by Labour's black hole. It is a question which has taken a long time to be asked, and even longer to be answered. But now two major political events have swept away the political life-support machinery which had hitherto prevented such a question being even posed.

The first, the collapse of communism, has had a silent but devastasting effect on Labour's confidence. It is not that many activists wanted a Bolshevik state established in Britain, but rather, that the Soviet régime acted as a beacon for those believing in Utopian politics. Here was an example not only of a Utopian ideal translated into day-to-day practice, but of a superstate motivated by a system of ethical judgement based around rewards – each according to his ability, each according to his needs. The Soviet régime collapsed almost overnight. Labour is taking a much longer time to adjust to the sweeping away of Utopian politics.

Secondly, Labour has at the same time suffered a series of major electoral rebuffs with which the Party has still to come to terms. At first senior party figures believed that the loss of power, while regrettable, was part of a normal course of events in the two-party system. That view is still mightily represented in some parts of the Party hierarchy and expresses itself around the idea that one more heave will restore Labour to power.

The results of the last four elections were not solely about the electorate embracing the Conservative cause. Equally important has been the electorate's rejection of the kind of socialism Labour was offering. An economy with core industries nationalized, a highly centralized government machine (although not nearly as centralized as the Thatcher Governments proved themselves to be) run on the basis of a compact with the trade unions, is not now the formula for successful electoral politics. Most of the activists in the country know this to be true, but some of the party's hierarchy is slow to adapt to the political facts of life. The key question is what should replace Labour's traditional appeal which has so often emphasized institutions rather than values.

This political life-support machinery – of believing that a Utopian solution to British political and economic problems was at hand, and that a swing back to Labour is inevitable – now needs to be switched off. Labour must answer the fundamental question of what it believes in.

In doing so, it must face the reality that, for at least the forseeable future, no party is going to get elected which is against the market economy. Here is the crunch. Is Labour going to embrace the market economy or not? At the moment the Party's position is ambivalent. Labour mouths statements in support of the market principle but all the Party's body language speaks of a deep distrust.

The market economy must be embraced without reservation. It works too well for too many people for too much of the time for any alternative to be practical politics. It is responsible for the highest standard of living known to mankind. It is inextricably bound up with a free society. Why then, if the advantages of the market economy are so obvious, is Labour diffident about embracing its principles?

Here again the answer is quite simple. For the whole of my political life Labour has espoused a view of human nature which is simply wrong. The self-regarding side of the human character has been ignored or suppressed. The result has meant a shaping of politics which not merely ignores self-interest, but goes out of its way to punish it. Self-interest is one of the most powerful of human characteristics and practical politics has to be built around that simple but fundamental fact. Moreover, it is through a market economy that self-interest can operate most easily to greatest effect and for the greatest common good.

That doesn't mean that the exercise of an unadulterated self-interest is always edifying, let alone acceptable, or that self-interest is the only consideration which society must take into account. What it does mean is that radical politics is about channelling self-interest wherever possible so that it also promotes the common good.

The agenda for radical politics for the next decade or more is one of attempting to deal with the unacceptable faces of the market economy. What those unacceptable faces are is dealt with at some length in this book. Instead of exhibiting a body language which most voters read as an expression of opposition to the market, Labour should embrace the market and spend the whole of its effort expressing its disapproval of the market's unacceptable faces – particularly its inability to tackle unemployment and its power to punish the poor and the least strong. The radical agenda is about eradicating these unacceptable faces without undermining the essential principles of the market. Here Labour's ethical tradition of socialism can come to the fore.

That ethical tradition has always consisted of two clear strands. The first, which has often been overshadowed, has been about the opening up of opportunities so that individuals (rather than classes) can develop and use their talents to the full. The second strand of the tradition is concerned with the protection and enhancement of the poor, the weak and the disadvantaged. It is here that Labour can play its strongest card. For the market economy left to itself is at best amoral. Labour's ethical tradition, built around the importance that should be attached to each individual member of the community, can provide the moral framework within which a more just market economy can flourish.

Merely to espouse the first principle – of ensuring the widest possible extension of opportunity to individuals to use their talents to the full – immediately suggests a whole range of policies, from action against unemployment right through to education reform. It is important that the development of policies on these fronts should be within the moral framework which is part of the Party's heritage. The emphasis on each individual will give a coherence to the Party's manifesto, while at the same time presenting the policies themselves with a much clearer cutting edge. The attack on unemployment, for example, is not urgent merely because of the lost production which results from it, or the added social problems which undoubtedly arise because of it. The task is urgent because unemployment is an attack on the sacredness of each unemployed individual. The existence of unemployment is a reminder of another important political fact. Contributing to, as well as receiving from, society must be given its proper weight in public policy. Today's unemployment prevents millions of people from making their rightful contribution to society, thereby gaining equal status to those in work.

Tackling unemployment effectively is at the heart of the 'vision thing' for British politics.

CHAPTER ONE

Reinventing the Traditional Party of Opposition

In *The Importance of Being Earnest* what Lady Bracknell said of Ernest's loss of both his parents could also be said about the losing of elections. If the loss of one election is unfortunate, and two careless, then three is reckless, four criminal, and to lose five in succession might well prove fatal. This chapter looks at the reasons for Labour's losing streak. It considers whether the Party is now so enfeebled that it will be unable to win again, unless it offers an electoral reform which will ensure that it is unlikely ever to form a one-party government again. The promise of electoral reform must be accompanied by the most fundamental changes in the Party's constitution if Labour is to continue to be a serious political force.

Rationalizing defeat

Whatever the result of the 1992 election, records were bound to be broken. For Labour to have won would have required a larger swing than had ever occurred in any previous election. For the Tories to win meant a record of four election victories in a row, a feat never achieved by a modern political party. Both the major parties, therefore, went into the record books – Labour by doing worse than any other party had done previously by losing four consecutive elections; the Conservatives simply by doing the opposite.

Why did Labour lose so easily and by such a wide margin? The twenty-one-seat Tory majority over all other parties disguises the extent of Labour's defeat. The Tory lead over

Labour in the popular vote was a staggering 7.5 percentage points. Labour cannot this time make its usual cry of 'we was robbed' by the electoral system. The unfairness of the voting system is not working against Labour. Had Labour cornered merely half a percentage point more of the popular vote the Tories, still with a 7 percentage point lead, would have been denied an overall majority in the House of Commons. Tactical voting played its part in the final result. Despite the commonly held view that only the Liberal Democrats gain from tactical voting, Labour was a main beneficiary, almost halving Mr Major's overall majority as a consequence.

What explanations have been put forward to account for Labour's dismal record? Here I group the main arguments under four headings, starting first with the considered views of psephologists.

Psephologists

Anthony Heath, Roger Jowell and John Curtice explain Labour's electoral failure not so much in terms of people switching sides, although that was what in part happened, as of the shrinking of the working-class base from which Labour has always drawn its main support. The size of the working-class population has fallen dramatically over the past two decades – by a sixth since 1971 – but even so this argument by itself is inadequate.

While the Heath thesis goes some way to explaining the long-term decline of Labour's vote, it has nothing to say on the reasons why people from traditional Labour-voting families came to believe that Labour no longer adequately represented their aspirations. These families may not define themselves as working class any more, but their economic circumstances are not so different from those of other families who, also experiencing significant changes in their living standards, continue to vote Labour.

Closely allied to the Heath thesis is one centered on class

conflict, the great exponents of which are psephologists David Butler and Donald Stokes. Their thesis is that, not surprisingly, a class-based appeal does well in times of clear class antagonism and vice versa.

It is hard not to recognize what Butler and Stokes write from conversations had on people's doorsteps, where a fundamental feeling of 'them and us' helps to determine the votes of some households. It works both ways, of course, with Tory voters having a mirror image of the 'them and us' spectrum. But does the thesis adequately explain Labour's long-term decline or does it point to other processes at work? The Butler/Stokes data highlight a decline in class antagonism and so one would expect, if they are right, to see Labour's vote similarly fall. Yet in the late 1960s when, according to the authors, class antagonism peaked leading one to expect Labour to do particularly well, the Party was unexpectedly defeated by Edward Heath. Class antagonism appears to have been replaced by a more widely diffused political antagonism to the Labour Party by no less than 65 per cent of voters.

Similarly, Professor Ivor Crewe's explanation accounts for only some of the main events. His thesis is that the working class is disintegrating from within as people no longer see themselves as working class, no longer propagate working-class values and, as a consequence, view themselves as Conservative voters.

The 1992 result did not prove the Crewe view entirely correct. There was a 1 per cent swing against the Labour Party from its supposed core working-class supporters, while a 4 per cent swing was notched up amongst the AB groups. Again, what Crewe describes, unsatisfactorily as a complete answer, is obvious to anyone who regularly canvasses in the same area over longish periods of time.

One other explanation of Labour's failed voting appeal rests on a belief about how voters perceive the likely course of the economy, and how self-interest is related to its developments – what the American economist John Kenneth Galbraith calls the 'culture of contentment'.

Conventional wisdom used to be that Oppositions not only could but probably would win when the economy was doing badly, causing concern to people about what the Government's economic mismanagement might cost them in reduced living standards. The 1992 election was fought during a slump as severe as the 1930s with real disposable income falling between 1990 and 1991. Yet, despite this traditional reasoning, Labour failed to win.

In contrast to this James Alt asserts that only if people feel economically secure will they risk voting Labour. But the Alt line has a degree of incongruity absent from all other explanations of Labour's electoral failure. Is it really believable that individuals will vote for a party on the basis that they are now well off enough to make themselves less well off by a government's mismanagement of the economy? There may be here a partial explanation of the feeling of some affluent voters about the prospect of tax increases. But I would be surprised if most of this group did not wish to be on the receiving end of rising living standards over the life of a Labour government, even if they paid back in part for those improved conditions in increased taxation. That view, however, is somewhat different from the proposition advanced by Alt.

The Contented Culture of Conservatism

The latest explanation, not merely of Labour's unelectability, but of the failure of radical parties in Europe and America, comes from the pen of J. K. Galbraith. After Labour's 1992 defeat commentators fell like vultures upon Galbraith's culture of contentment thesis. His line is as simple as it is eloquently expressed. Two-thirds of the electorate have a vested interest in the economic and therefore political status quo. Radical parties intent on redistributing to the underdog do not get elected. No sooner had Galbraith collected his royalties than this idea ran into the buffers of Bill Clinton's election win.

What are the politician and voter supposed to make of

these varying explanations of Labour's failure to achieve a decisive breakthrough? And what lessons should Labour draw from the Clinton campaign?

Many of the psephologists step carefully around the obvious reason why Labour falters when voters have to decide on polling day. From the very start, and long before universal franchise, political parties in this country have been about representing interests. A major part of a political party's function is to set out a stall which is attractive enough in representing interests and aspirations so that enough voters become regular customers.

The word 'aspirations' is important. I believe we are now in a transitional stage where the electoral system has moved on from simply representing major economic interests. To some extent, of course, that still applies. Traditionally, Labour represents what voters perceive as the interests of the working class and the underdog. But a majority of voters are not sufficiently attracted by such a slate alone to vote in a Labour government. Indeed, many people who would be classified by occupation as working class find Labour's programme positively unattractive.

Labour's representation of interests has an essentially static approach. For much of its existence the Party has been making an appeal to the voters when politicians were unappreciative of the effects that economic growth not only would have but was having on political aspirations. Wave upon wave of workers were made unemployed during the 1920s and 1930s. The fight was essentially to get out of this pit. Labour's solution was socialism, which one day would rectify the injustices. Until then the struggle of opposing capitalism would continue and, because most working families were aware of what life would be like if their wage packet was denied them, Labour's collective approach to security had a powerful appeal.

This approach went unquestioned even though during the 1930s many working-class families – particularly those in the South – were the grateful beneficiaries of economic growth.

Living standards of those in work rose during that decade. Labour's incompetence during the 1929–1931 Government was overshadowed by the world slump. Blaming as traitors Labour ministers who helped form the National Government was easier than looking for more deep-seated causes of such poor political performance which most Labour leaders thought would take two post-war elections to rectify. The sweepstake amongst Labour leaders guessing the 1945 result was won on an estimate of a 40-seat Tory majority. That guess was the closest to the actual result of a Labour majority over the Conservatives of 196 seats.

The first hint of a possible divergence of traditional class interests and the newly emerging aspirations of voters began to register during that first post-war government. The ration-book approach of fair shares lost its appeal. Much more popular was 'the bonfire of restrictions' which, to his credit, Harold Wilson instigated as President of the Board of Trade. But it was left to the Tories to make the most out of the determination to do away with wartime restrictions and rationing. In one of those decisive electoral junctures, in 1951, the Conservatives impressed upon the voter's mind that they sided with those who wanted the freedom to get on and build their own lives.

A similar political juncture came at the end of the 1970s. Racked by the shift in economic power to the oil producers, those in work tried to prevent the resulting inflation from cutting living standards as this global transfer of wealth took effect. The stage was being set for another of those once-in-a-generation shifts in the political debate. The issue and the moment came together in the sale of council houses. I develop this point because the significance of this issue is still underrated by practitioners and commentators alike. Of course it was an immediate vote winner. But it had equally important long-term effects on British politics.

The Primacy of Home Ownership

The sale of council houses appears to have had a lasting influence on how the Labour and Conservative parties are perceived by many of the electorate to a degree which most political commentators have missed. When in 1976 I advocated that Labour should be the party of 'freeing the council house serfs', I was addressing how best politicians could persuade people to devote more of their income to covering housing costs. The only way I believed this possible was to change the rules: hence the option to buy. Only partially did I perceive the long-term political importance of the sales policy. I realized, of course, it was an election winner which could be ours, but I did not then comprehend how one single policy could so symbolize a party's link with the future. While Labour embroiled itself in vicious internal warfare, the Tories went out to meet the future.

Council house sales have an appeal which extends beyond council house tenants themselves. No policy statement or action comes anywhere near to having the almost sacramental impact this policy has had on what political parties stand for. While the Conservatives scooped the advantages of espousing freedom, Labour's fractious opposition to the sale of council houses made an equally indelible mark on the electorate. Increasingly, Labour was seen as a party looking backwards and wanting to hold people down. A decade and more after the mass sale of council houses became a political reality, the NEC report on the 1992 election continued to record key voters perceiving Labour as the party of the past.

Council house sales affected the political debate in a second decisive way. It was the issue on which the voters' aspirations took primacy over class interests. I need to go back again to the 1950s bonfire of controls.

The return to government of the Conservatives in 1950 saw the dismantling of wartime industrial controls. The effects on supplies to the shops, which occurred after the dismantling of controls and regulations, had a wide appeal, not least to those who experienced the drudgery of the 1930s and the hardships of the 1940s. Goods slowly became more available and the end of coupons signalled the demise of the spivs and the black market. The market system which Labour held in such disdain seemed to be working. This was, however, change within old structures. Life went on very much the same. Those who could worked five and a half days a week for fifty weeks of each year.

The sale of council houses came at a time when rising living standards had reached a point when many ordinary individuals could start making decisive choices over how they spent their growing leisure hours. Non-working hours grew in importance both in their length and in the opportunities they offered individuals.

People were opting for their own form of privatization long before Mrs Thatcher began shifting around industrial ownership from public to private monopolies. The most significant visible sign of this came in the inexorable climb in the number and percentage of people owning their homes. The figures rocketed under the Conservative Government's sales policy. Through their own home, and their leisure pursuits, voters were building their own world which ruthlessly excluded officialdom. While public services remained important, an increasing priority was given to private pastimes. Tax rates thereby took on a new significance. It wasn't simply a matter of wishing to pay for a pukka health service. That demand now competed with resources which might be spent on a new kitchen, bathroom, extension or in planning regular family holidays.

It was the Conservatives who became seen in the voter's mind as the party which not only understood this new development, but which encouraged it. Council house sales therefore have to be seen as a second stage in the Tories' 1950 appeal of being the party which abolished controls, freed business, which began the age of mass consumption. Here the cry of 'setting the people free' was immeasurably reinforced with a 'trust the people' approach. The policy reinforced the

Tory message that they were on the side of the individual. Labour's stance did the opposite.

The difference between the parties could not have been clearer during the last election. One of the Prime Minister's more important speaking engagements was at a DIY store. Labour's spin-doctors snobbishly laughed at his performance. On polling day that laugh appeared on other faces. Significantly, the DIY appearance was not engineered by the pollsters: It was a natural event for a party which shared the aspiring lifestyles of a growing majority of voters. These aspirations are now forming a new block of consumer interests in politics which has to operate within a two-party system.

Labour's Self-destruction

While the Conservatives were confirming their role as enhancers of individual freedom, Labour, though unintentionally, spent its efforts in making the Party as unattractive as possible. It was not long after the 1979 defeat that Labour fell into a lengthy bout of ethnic cleansing of those in the Party who were deemed not to be true socialists. These actions by the Bennite praetorian guard have done lasting damage to the Labour Party which it is hard to underestimate. The ranting and screaming, and the guard's use of verbal abuse, were seen too often on television for it not to have entered the subconscious of many voters. Again, in contrast to the Conservative's action of being on the side of the voters, Labour offered the image of the bully.

The immediate damage brought about by these actions was evident in the 1983 result. Indeed, it is possible to argue that Labour, far from being damaged electorally by the SDP's secession, was saved from an almost complete electoral rout by the existence of this new party. The SDP gave hordes of Labour voters a convenient non-Tory safe haven in that election. Without the SDP candidates, and their Liberal colleagues, many Labour voters would have shown their contempt for what was happening within the Labour Party by crossing straight over to the Tories. As it was, many did. Even with the existence of a third party attachment, the 1983 result was worse than the disastrous 1931 election.

Time is running out. How many more elections can we lose and still expect Labour voters to remain loyal? The Asquithian Liberals found to their astonishment, and anger, how quickly voters move once they see a viable alternative. The build up of Liberal Democrat councillors – doubling over the decade – and the capturing of local government seats in by-elections on a scale which outpaces both the Conservative and Labour Parties combined is an ominous warning. Moreover, at the time of writing, it is a year after the election and no serious discussion has begun on the lessons we must draw from a record-breaking series of defeats.

So what can be done? I use the remainder of this chapter to sketch out an answer on four key issues for Labour's future. These are first, why it is urgent for Labour to become an effective challenger for power even if that challenge has to be accomplished in union with Liberal Democrats; second, why even in this context Labour's political programme matters; third, what lessons are there to be learnt from Bill Clinton's success in the United States; and, fourth, what kind of party must Labour be for enough of the electorate ever to trust it with sharing power?

An Effective Opposition

First there is the question of why Labour must get itself into a credible position to challenge for power. I cannot impress enough the importance which the fear of losing power has in checking abuses of government. Take any one week of John Major's Government's existence and examples can be found of what I mean. It appears that anything is now permissible and nothing is so serious as to warrant resignation. Being a spectator for the last fourteen years leads me to the conclusion that it is a fear of electoral defeat which is the most powerful check we have in our democratic system. Offering programmes of constitutional change, however exciting they are to the political élite, is no substitute for winning power. Indeed, the constitutional caravan which now meanders over British politics is itself largely a product of Labour's failure to win power. Without winning power, constitutional plans remain mere plans.

The issue on which I want to focus is Labour's traditional commitment to the poor and the underdog. For two reasons it is now more not less important to see that these views are effectively represented. It is of course a harder job now. The poor are in a minority, and the terms 'poor' and 'working class', used for so much of Labour's existence as if they were synonymous, are no longer.

The poor are out there on their own. I will not stress the figures here; I set them out in the next chapter when I look at the opportunities for Labour which come as a by-product of Tory policy. Few doubt that the gap between the poor and what is called the average family has widened decisively under Mrs Thatcher's stewardship. It would be surprising if it hadn't; it was, after all, an object of government policy.

Towards the end of her long life Beatrice Webb was asked what was the most significant change she had observed during her lifetime. Unhesitatingly she replied that it was the disappearance of beggars from Britain's streets. Beggars are now back in force once again. But they are not an isolated social group. They are the tip of a huge social iceberg. The beggars are part of a continuum embracing literally millions of our fellow citizens, many of whom are hidden from our sight. The Thatcher Government went about the largest redistribution of wealth to the rich that has ever been recorded in this country. As a result of this redistribution, rising unemployment, the reduction in benefits for some and outright abolition for groups of teenagers, we should not be surprised that beggars are now very much in evidence. As Mrs Thatcher might have said, you cannot buck all these moves by government and survive.

Never before have the needs of the poor required greater representation than now, and never before has Labour been less able to fulfil this role. To do so Labour has to win, and that brings us back firmly again to policies which meet people's aspirations. In the following chapters I deal with this in some detail. Here I wish only to emphasize the importance of a political programme.

Programmes Matter

Elections in the past have of course been won without any definite programme being put forward by the winning side. But since Labour is no longer seen by the majority of the electorate as a serious competitor for power, the importance of a programme to win over new voters is crucial. Only by remoulding itself around a programme which raises hopes and aspirations and is seen to work with, rather than against, the grain of human nature, does the Party stand any chance of increasing its share of the vote at the next election. In creating that chance, policy has a fundamental part to play.

We need here to take a leaf out of Mrs Thatcher's book. In inducing voters into a new mould, Mrs Thatcher designed a programme targeted to that end. The liberal intelligentsia may have viewed Mrs Thatcher's Conservative Party with disdain, but large numbers of voters did not. It is often forgotten now, but in 1974 commentators saw Labour as the natural party of government and were busily writing off the Conservatives as a totally spent political force.

From 1975 onwards Mrs Thatcher went out to remould what the Conservative Party stood for. In those crucial four years prior to the 1979 contest Mrs Thatcher and her team began to build a programme which created the politico-intellectual sea change which only in the closing stages of the 1979 Election campaign Jim Callaghan realized was about to engulf him and the Labour Government. If Labour is to have any chance in staving off a fifth successive election defeat similar determination, vision, and simple hard work must now, at this stage of the parliament, be undertaken.

Here Labour's Commission on Social Justice comes into view. That Labour should be undertaking the most wide-ranging review of social policy is not in question: the timing is. The Commission is working to a two-year timetable. Though it will be publishing papers and reports along the way, its findings will not be published until well into the second half of this parliament. The ideas it proposes will then have to be discussed with rank and file members before the Party can adopt and campaign around a new strategy.

If the commission comes up with radical proposals they will need selling to the electorate. A strategy that leaves the new policy under dust sheets, so to speak, and unexplained to the electorate, is unlikely to work. Not only is the electorate likely to feel that it is being hoodwinked by such a strategy, but such an operation misreads the task before the Labour Party. We are not attempting to regain power after a temporary relapse. The party has suffered not one but a whole series of major rebuffs at the hands of the electorate. In *Sans Everything* the old man is being shaken by an angry nurse. He replies: 'It take time to die nurse, it takes time nurse.' Similarly, it takes even longer not to prevent a political death but to stage a successful comeback. Policy changes this time round are not about picking up a few floating voters along the way, welcome as this would be. They need to be about convincing political opponents amongst the electorate that the Party has fundamentally changed, which takes time and much explaining. That is precisely what Mrs Thatcher did and she was duly rewarded. In contrast, Labour appears to be adopting an approach in which policy will be unveiled at the last possible moment.

The US Example

The third issue I want to consider is what lessons can usefully be learned from the United States. Much nonsense is talked about whether Labour has anything at all to learn from

34

Clinton. On this I make one comment. If an international seminar on political success were being organized, Clinton would receive an invitation, Labour would not.

Learning from the United States takes the discussion onto reforming the Labour Party itself, which has to accompany any change in the programme the Party puts forward. In drawing on the US experience it is important to underline the differences between our two political cultures. But these differences, significant as they are, should not swamp the similarities, the most important of which was that in 1992 the Democratic Party was, as the Labour Party is, a party with a tradition of losing elections.

It is important, of course, not to misread or misunderstand the basis of Clinton's election success. There is the crucial economic difference in the performance of the American economy in the run up to the 1992 election and the economic background to the last three Conservative victories in this country. Although real disposable income fell in this country between 1990 and 1991, it had increased by seventy per cent over the previous twenty years. In contrast, the standard of living of many Americans, and particularly the Democratic Republicans, which was one of the keys to the Reagan and Bush victories, suffered a decline. For all but the richest fifth, incomes stagnated in the 1980s. Families with below-average incomes actually saw pay-packets shrink by almost three per cent in the second half of the decade. Such a decline was unheard of and the dent it put in millions of Americans' aspirations contributed crucially to the Democrats' win. In Britain, by contrast, wages and salaries generally kept above the rate of inflation.

But Clinton did not sideline himself, or his party, waiting for an economic crisis to win the election. One is tempted to believe that, while the Major Central Office team was busy advising Bush on his electoral tactics, Mrs Thatcher was similarly getting Clinton to understand the basis of her success. Unlike any previous political leader, Mrs Thatcher went out from the very start in 1975 to convince the electorate that she had turned her back on the record of previous Tory administrations, not least that in which she was one of the biggest spenders. The strategy worked. As the voters came up to the election tape in 1979 enough saw the Tory Party under Mrs Thatcher as having discarded what was seen by many as the discredited concensus politics of the last three decades which appeared to so many to be resulting in chaos.

Whether advised by Mrs Thatcher or not, Clinton applied an equal determination to destroy his links with the old, traditional Democratic Party as it fought the presidential election. The Party, of course, continued to be successful in many state, local and congressional elections. Indeed he went even further than Mrs Thatcher: he made a virtue out of apologizing for the Party's past. Contrast this with the British record. All the changes Neil Kinnoock wrought in the Labour Party were presented as though nothing much had happened, or, at best, that any such changes were only a logical extension of previously long-held positions. Big changes were made but the voters would be forgiven in thinking that they weren't. Bigger changes remain to be made.

Democratic leaders have distinct advantages over their Labour counterparts. Presidential candidates emerge through a public primary system where voters choose a candidate whose programme reflects their views. Changing a party programme is therefore that much easier. Change is also made easier since the Democratic Party is a much looser federation than the British Labour Party. Moreover, vested interests are not built into the day-to-day running of the Party as they are in the Labour Party.

But Clinton did not leave the matter of the Democratic Party's past failure by making a general apology. Unlike Labour, Clinton did not blame the voters. He laid the blame squarely on the Party. Instead of pretending that those voters with different views to the Party's prevailing orthodoxy were a collection of moral deviants, Clinton went out, met and listened to the voters. The Democratic programme this time began and ended with the fears and hopes, despair and aspirations of voters who had previously crossed over to the Republicans.

There is another equally important lesson to learn from Clinton's success. This centres on his insistence on building up a programme which appealed to a wide coalition of interests and brought the Democrat Party diverse support. What might be done in the UK on this score is an underlying theme of all the following chapters.

Here I underline the importance of the apology Clinton gave to the voters for the past behaviour of the Democrat Party. Labour must similarly seek the opportunities and the occasions to gain a *rapprochement* with the electorate.

Party Reform

An apology in words has to be followed with action and here I begin with the nature of the Labour Party itself. If what happened in the early 1980s had occurred to an individual we would have classified the event as a severe mental breakdown. It is not enough for Labour to apologize and promise to do better, although that would be a start. Two decisive changes must take place. A commitment to changing the voting system should accompany a total overhaul of the Party's constitution. The Party structure must be reformed to prevent a situation from occurring again where pressure from minority groups results in a large part of the Party leadership commending to voters views and policies which, without that pressure, they have since recanted.

The greatest defence of our current electoral system is that it produces strong government. But consider for a moment what is meant by strong. If pushing through a programme about which many back-benchers on the government's side have major reservations is a sign of strength, then I suppose the British Government qualifies. Similarly, if a strong government is equated with the views of only a minority of the electorate being imposed upon the majority, then again Britain can claim that it is ruled by a strong government.

But if the words 'strong government' are dropped in favour of 'representative government', then our voting system does far less well – indeed it does very badly. Take the 1992 election results. If two parties are wiped out completely from the calculations, the distribution of seats almost exactly mirrors the proportion of votes gained in the country. The two parties which need to disappear from consideration are the Liberal Democrats and the Scottish Nationalists whose following in the country was not represented by the number of seats they held in the House of Commons.

My belief is that the declaration of a willingness to change the electoral system and, if need be, to share power with another party might – just – so restore Labour with the electorate that it wins an outright majority to implement such a programme. But the price is high. The chances of this working have to be weighed against the possibility that Labour might never again form a majority government.

A promise to reform the electoral system needs also to be accompanied by determined shake-up of the Party's own constitution. As action here can take place without winning an election, change on this front gives a glorious opportunity for the Party to convince voters that it has not only been transformed, but is prepared to take the kinds of tough decisions with respect to its own domain which will be even more necessary with respect to the country after the next general election.

We need to start with an acceptance that the so-called democratic reforms of the Party in the early 1980s were largely undesirable; they concentrated power in the hands of the activists rather than the full membership. It is also necessary to accept that we live in an age of privatized leisure which is hostile to the 'public meeting' syndrome which political parties are dependent upon. So let me end by listing the agenda as I see it for party reform. This agenda rejects proposals such as giving every levy-paying trade union member full Labour Party membership. It calls for an end to the block vote in the running of party affairs. An age which sees the end of mass parties calls for a new constitution to match the times in which we live.

Indeed, a hundred years since its first constitution was established Labour should seize the opportunity to draft a new constitution. Amongst many changes, the new constitution should state that the parliamentary leader – the person who would become prime minister – should be elected by Members of Parliament only. The present electoral college system prevents any leader from being removed from office against his or her wishes – that needs to end. Also voters don't want trade unions to have a say in who is going to be the prime minister as they elect MPs directly to make that choice.

Second, a position of party president should be created which would be elected on a one person–one vote membership throughout the entire Party. The party president would have the task of supporting the Party in the country and representing those views in the shadow cabinet. The holder would carry shadow cabinet rank irrespective of whether he or she was an MP or peer.

Third, trade union members should have an influence in the Party only to the extent to which individual trade unionists chose to carry Party cards. The block vote would therefore be abolished.

Fourth, as Labour will never have a mass membership, the Party should therefore cut its organizational cloak according to this cloth. The efforts of regional organizers and their staff at the last election helped secure twice the national average swing in some key marginal constituencies. That success needs to be spread and reflected in the balance of staff between Labour's headquarters at Walworth Road and the regions. A party which preaches decentralization and regionalism as the basis for reforming British government would justly get short shrift from the electorate if it maintained a rigid centralization of power in its own affairs.

Fifth, the preparation of policy documents should fall to the staff in the Leader of the Opposition's office, and the offices of trade unions. Trade unions, as affiliated organizations, would have a right to present policy proposals at the NEC and at the national conference. Conference should become a forum for debate rather than pretending it is some form of representative parliament – which it clearly is not. The adoption of policy should be by the membership by postal ballot. This would affect how the trade unions vote in the Party. The trade union vote in Party affairs would be limited to the number of real, rather than imaginary, Labour Party members contained by the unions. Those members would need to pay the full membership and not gain influence because they pay the political levy.

Sixth, the selection of parliamentary candidates would be by one person–one vote only. Re-selections would be initiated by a majority vote of all constituency party members.

Seventh, Clause 4 Part 4 of the existing constitution (which demands common ownership of the means of production, distribution and exchange) would be omitted, giving Labour the chance to express its objectives adequately. Labour's ends are not about the dreary task of nationalizing or renationalizing this or that industry. Over half of British industry is already owned by the voters through their pension funds (how to make this ownership effective is considered in the fifth chapter). In the place of Clause 4 Part 4 Labour's view of ethical socialism should be proclaimed. Our central challenge is about how to create a society where self-interest is balanced by a proper emphasis on fellowship. Our central task is to formulate varying policies which will allow the poorest the opportunites to develop their talents which are equal to those of the richest. Our central difficulty will be in rewarding adequately those with the greatest talents while cherishing those whose talents are less prized by the market.

In the early 1980s Labour promised to bring about an irreversible shift of wealth and power to ordinary people.

That objective must first be enshrined in the Party's new constitution if voters are to elect a Labour government. The constitution, through the one person–one vote principle, must ensure, above all, that the ordinary Party members hold the decisive say in what the Party stands for and how it should go about achieving its objectives.

Conclusion

Despite the Government's chronic unpopularity, Labour looks as though it may have been beached by the electorate. But the beaching is not of a kind which makes it obvious that the Party can never win again. Between elections the tide comes in and laps around the stranded ship. But that tide never comes in far enough to lift the Party free and sweep it out to an election victory. Similarly, because the crew can see the tide lapping around the boat it remains loyal in the hope that, this time, the tide of disgust against the Government will somehow lift their boat free. By remaining at their post the crew are not engaged in building an alternative, more streamlined craft which could sail the electoral tides.

Part of the crew's time must be spent in showing the electorate that the boat is once again seaworthy. Two reforms above all else are necessary to achieve this objective. First, the Party must pledge itself to reforming the electoral system. This would require a public declaration to the effect that the Party may never be presented with power on its own again, other than to deliver a change in the voting system. To continue the metaphor, Labour will need the help of another craft if it is to be pulled free of the electoral mudbank on which it has been stranded since 1979. Accompanying this pledge on voting reform, the Party must draw up a new constitution enshrining the one person–one vote principle. It must also have a clear statement of objectives which, as Jack Straw has wryly noted, can be proudly shown to voters rather than shamefacedly hidden from view.

CHAPTER TWO

Reclaiming Labour's Natural Constituency

The politics of the Thatcher governments are commented upon in a manner which suggests that they have made Labour irrelevant to a permanent majority of the electorate. This chapter examines why and how this has happened. It looks at the fiscal redistribution brought about by Mrs Thatcher which itself explains why a growing proportion of the population are living on low incomes. The extent of this success now offers radicals their opportunity to win. While significant in number, the poor are still very clearly a minority. The Thatcher governments persuaded many commentators (some didn't need persuading) that the poor were a forgotten cause: 'There are no votes there.' If a more careful analysis of the distribution of income in the post-Thatcher age were to be carried out, a potentially larger grouping of voters would be found who could be mobilized by policies based on Labour's traditional values. Such policies must be presented in a manner which appeals to the aspirations of these voters.

Tax Cuts Galore

Two trends in taxes have been evident since 1979, as the table opposite illustrates. Reduction in taxation is calculated by assuming that the 1978–79 tax regime has continued unmodified. From the level of taxation that this would have produced is deducted the current tax yields. The result shows the level of taxation has been cut in this current year by a simply astonishing total of £31.4 billion. We know that the rich gained most from these tax cuts, but the extent of their gains will surprise many.

Average reduction in income tax per individual in 1992–93 compared with the 1978–79 indexed regime[1]

Range of individuals income in 1992–93 £	Number of individuals 1992–93[1] Million	Total reduction £ Million	Average reduction £ per annum
Under 5,000	3.1	500	150
5,000 to 10,000	7.9	3,200	400
10,000 to 15,000	6.2	4,500	730
15,000 to 20,000	4.1	4,300	1,060
20,000 to 30,000	3.2	5,000	1,590
30,000 to 50,000	1.2	3,600	2,960
50,000 to 80,000	0.35	3,100	9,200
Over 80,000	0.15	7,200	46,000
TOTAL	26.2	31,400	1,200

[1] Individuals liable to income tax under the 1978–79 indexed regime.

Hansard, 29 June 1992, col. 4 (W)

The richest taxpayers, those earning over £80,000 a year, shared a total of £7.2 billion. Their numbers total 150,000. Their average tax reduction since 1979 amounts to £46,000. The cumulative increase in income resulting from the Tory tax changes for the richest 0.5 per cent of taxpayers was larger than the original income of the bottom 87 per cent of taxpayers.

Those with income between £50,000 and £80,000 in the current tax year – 350,000 taxpayers – gained individual tax reductions since 1979 averaging £9,200. The richest taxpayers, less than 2 per cent, therefore cornered over a third of all tax reductions since 1979.

Those earning between £5,000 and £10,000 a year – 7.9 million taxpayers in all, the largest single group in the entire distribution – gained tax reductions of £3.2 billion or, on average, £400 since 1979. The very poorest taxpayers, those with incomes under £5,000 a year, who total 3.1 million, gained £0.5 billion in income tax reduction, or individually, a total tax reduction of £150 spread over the years since 1979.

Wage Cuts Galore

Tax cuts have not been the only force at work generating greater inequality. Changes in the basic distribution of income have also had a dramatic effect on its overall distribution of income. The outcome of these changes can be considered from three different perspectives – what people receive from working; how the shares of income, including unearned income, have changed; and the extent to which the distribution of pre-tax income has been affected by taxation.

First, what have been the changes in the distribution of income from work? It would be surprising if no changes were recorded over the period since 1979. Much government effort has been given to dismantling employment protection laws and this, together with the increase in the numbers of unemployed, has had a major impact on reducing what were already low wages. The time limit for protection against unfair dismissal has been raised from six months to two years. The right to arbitration in pay disputes has been abolished; unfair dismissal procedures have been relaxed; the Fair Wages Resolution has been abolished; the wages council machinery, which enacts minimum wages for 2.5 million of the lowest paid workers, has been weakened; and half a million of the youngest workers have been removed from its protection altogether. By the time this book is published the Government will have piloted a Bill through Parliament abolishing the wages council machinery in its entirety. It is hardly surprising that the combination of freeing the labour market in these ways (as the Government likes euphemistically to call it) and the impact of rising unemployment for most of the last decade has increased the number of workers on low wages.

Here are two measurements of this change. The Council of Europe sets what is called a 'decency threshold', currently of £5.15 an hour. In 1979 7.8 million British workers were below what was then the equivalent threshold. By 1991 that total had risen to over 10 million, almost half (47 per cent) of those in employment.

The other important measurement here is to gauge the value of the wages of the lowest 10 per cent of workers against average earnings. In 1979 the value of the lowest male earnings measured against median earning was 66 per cent. By 1992 this had fallen to 57.5 per cent. When official pay records first commenced in 1886 the pay of the poorest 10 per cent was put at 66.6 per cent of median earnings.

The pay of the poorest women workers shows a similiar polarization. In 1979 the earnings of the poorest 10 per cent of women workers was 69.4 per cent of the median. By 1992 this had fallen to 61.1 per cent.

Abstract figures often fail to give an impression of just how low these wages are. Many of the cards in the Birkenhead jobcentre leave the section on pay blank, except for the phrase 'To be negotiated', or inform applicants that the pay is on a commission basis only. Here are four examples where employers have filled in the section on the level of wages offered, which indicate low-wage employment in Britain today.

● Local nursing home. Part-time night care assistant. 2 nights 10 to 8, experienced, over 21, caring for needs for 11 residents all night working on their own. Some domestic duties. £2.20 an hour.

● Security guard, part-time, must be numerate and literate. £2 an hour.

● Weekend cook. 9.30 to 5.30 to cook for 15 elderly residents. Total charge. £2.20 an hour.

- Dishwasher/kitchen assistant. Monday to Friday. 11 to 4.30. 18 plus, experienced preferred, £2.00 an hour.

Incomes On The March

The Dutch economist Jan Pen constructed in 1971 a verbal image of the inequality in income and wealth. A march past is arranged and the entire population is under orders to pass within an hour, the height of each person relating to their income. Recently *The Economist* reconstructed the Pen illustration so as to highlight the significant changes which have occurred in the distribution of income during this Tory Government's stewardship. Again the march past is planned to be completed in an hour.

As the imaginary procession begins the marchers are actually marching upside down. These are people with negative incomes who have lost money over the previous year. Although this part of the procession takes only a few seconds, it is twice as long as it was in 1970 because there are far more small businesses with a high failure rate. Soon the first marchers appear the right way up, but they are very small – it takes about five minutes before they are even a foot tall. Many of these dwarf-like figures are women, working part-time, although there are many more female midgets because one and a half times as many women work part-time now than they did in 1970. They are also marching with other midgets, such as single unemployed people. For nearly half of the fifth minute we see a stream of eleven 3/4 inch sixteen-year-olds collecting the same allowance on the Youth Training Scheme, whose 1970 equivalents in manual jobs and apprenticeships would have been about twice as tall. There are also some old faces in this part of the crowd, some of them pensioners, who in 1970 were fewer in number and were pushed further back in the queue.

After twenty minutes, the marchers are still less than three feet tall. The few that are in full-time work are mainly women

– shop assistants, cleaners and hairdressers. There are also unemployed family men and single mothers who collect benefit for themselves and their dependants.

After twenty-five minutes, most of the marchers are working, including men on full-time wages, doing farm labouring, portering and cleaning restaurants, hospitals and offices. These low-paid workers are in the same sorts of jobs as in 1970, and their height has remained almost constant, at a little under 4 feet, although some manual workers in local authority employment have shrunk.

Half-way through the march the marchers are still dwarves, and it is not until forty minutes have passed that people of average height (5 feet and 6 inches) appear. These average marchers are people in the lower-paid professions: secretaries, postmen and so on. As the last quarter of an hour begins we see teachers, some highly-paid manual workers, bank managers, executive-grade civil servants and policemen, who have grown around 19 inches since 1970.

As the end of the march approaches, the marchers' height increases rapidly. Only one tenth of those marching in the last ten minutes are women, and we see 10-foot journalists, 12-foot civil service principals, some barristers and consultants 10 or 15 yards high, and merchant bankers towering hundreds of feet into the air. Still, behind these giants come some of Britain's top executives, who reach as high as the New York World Trade Center; and in the last split second some of those whose income is derived from inherited wealth or unearned income, such as the Duke of Westminster, whose head is invisible, 20 miles above ground level.

Unemployment has had a double effect on the distribution of earnings. Unemployment has by its very nature driven many out of the labour market altogether. Others it has forced to take lower paid, often temporary, part-time jobs in order to stave off being drafted into Britain's conscript army of unemployed. The effect of rising unemployment – a fact of life since the mid-1960s, and particularly since 1979 – has therefore been part of the downward push on the wages of those at the bottom of the income pile. For while the poorest at work have fallen further behind those on average earnings, all the official data collected by the Government show that those in the highest paid positions have been drawing away from the average in an even more marked fashion. Unemployment has also, of course, affected the incomes of many people as they have been denied their wage packets and forced onto social security.

Redefining the Poor

Given this information, it will be of no surprise that the numbers of poor have shown a dramatic increase since 1979, although the Government objects to the use of that term. Mrs Thatcher put the objection thus:

> I have too much respect for ordinary people to belittle those who receive income support by the use of labels like 'poor'. I firmly believe that the best way to help *everyone* is through encouraging them to take pride in themselves and to make use of their talents rather than alienating them, making them feel helpless and encouraging dependency upon the state.

It is important to note that the Prime Minister shunned the term 'poor', not because poor people didn't exist, but in deference to their feeling. She is right, of course, in that we want people to take a pride in themselves and not collapse into what is known as the dependency culture. Refusing to use the term 'poor' is, in fact, an agreed Government line. We are invited instead to use the term low income. Two sets of data now exist from measurements taken of the numbers on low income. What picture do they paint?

Since the war taxpayers have provided a safety net benefit guaranteeing a minimum income to most of those unable to work. Originally it was termed National Assistance. In 1966 it was renamed Supplementary Benefit. And, since 1988, it has been called Income Support. A significant feature of the post-war period has been the steady rise in the number claiming this benefit. From 1948 to 1979 the numbers of claimants rose from one million to 2.9 million. By May 1991 this figure had risen to 4.5 million.

More dramatic still has been the number of people dependent upon this benefit – claimants plus their dependents. In 1948 this total stood at 1.5 million. By 1979 it had swollen to 4.4 million. Today it totals 7.7 million. The increase in the number of people dependent upon the safety net benefits in 1979 has therefore been greater than that experienced during the previous thirty years.

There are other people on very low incomes which should be added to these totals. Not everyone who is eligible to claim income support does so. Nor is everyone with an income below income support levels eligible for benefit. Those in full-time work for example are excluded.

In 1972 a special analysis was carried out on the Family Expenditure Survey (FES) in order to throw light on the size of these two groups. The findings were published under the title *Low-Income Families*. This analysis of FES data was carried out annually until 1979. In that year the Government announced that the data were to be analyzed and published only every other year. With the publication in 1988 of the 1985 data, the Government announced that the series would cease publication altogether. At this point the Commons' Select Committee on Social Security picked up the baton and began publishing its analysis of the FES data to continue the series on *Low Income Families*. What picture emerges from the post–1979 period?

In that year 3.17 million people were found to be living below the then Supplementary Benefit/Income Support level. This rose to 4 million in 1983, fell to 3.68 million in 1985 but then continued to climb in 1987 and reached 4.3 million in 1989. The numbers living at or below the safety net level of income stood at 11.37 million in 1989 (the last year for which we have data on both the numbers claiming benefit and the numbers living below the IS level).

In place of the low-income families data the Government substituted *Households Below Average Income*. The word household in the title is significant. Measuring groups by household – which generally encompasses more people than do data analyses on a family eligibility basis – lowers the number of individuals found to be living on low income. The Institute of Fiscal Studies calculates that this method of computation reduces the total on low income by around a million. But let the figures tell their own story.

The Government concentrates its attention, no doubt in the hope of directing the attention of others, to those living at below 50 per cent of average income. Following the Government's gaze, we see that in 1979 the numbers below this cut-off point stood at 3.75 million people. By 1989 this total had almost trebled to 10.4 million. The Government also strongly argues for the use of data compiled before housing costs began to be taken into account. That there is a case for considering income after housing costs is conceded by the Government in that it produces it in its own official papers.

The balance of argument here is fairly evenly struck. If people are reduced to low income, by part-time work or unemployment, they are unable in the short term to change their housing and thereby its costs. As housing costs are fixed, unlike other necessities such as food and heating, there is a case for data which look at the income levels after housing costs. The official figures of the latest available data calculated after housing costs are deducted show a rise from 4.93 million people living on income below half the average income in 1979 to 12 million people in 1989.

Whatever measurement is taken, from *Low Income Families* or *Households Below Average Income*, the picture is dismally similar. Not only are there large numbers of poor, or people on low income, but their numbers have risen dramatically under Conservative administration since 1979: twelve million people living in households with less than half the average income and 11.37 million people living at or below the minimum IS levels.

These figures, shocking as they are, ought not to be a surprise. As we have seen, a number of immensely powerful forces have been unleashed, and each is in its own right a powerful agent for inequality. A major aim of fiscal policy has been to redistribute tax revenue to the richest. Many of the Tory tax cuts have been paid for by abolishing benefits and cutting the rate of increase for many others. Total savings made by way of social security cuts are now estimated at over £40 billion. Freeing the Labour market has had a major downward impact on wage levels, as has a post-war record level of unemployment.

Disenfranchising the Poor

The poor have been vulnerable to each of these attacks. But other forces are at work undermining their position still further. The natural allies of the poor are now in a much weakened position. Labour has been powerless since 1979, and will remain so unless it is prepared to adopt the root and branch reforms which are being advocated. The Opposition can huff and bluff but such activities pay no part in shaping the policies of which the poor are on the receiving end. There was a time when Labour, seen as an effective challenger for power, could influence policy even though it was in opposition. That influence came from the very fact that, being a credible Opposition, the government was in fear of losing votes, and willing therefore to make important concessions. Indeed it is arguable that the close fought two-party struggle for power, and its resulting concensus, ensured that the most reactionary of policies were never brought forward in the first place.

Changes in the trade union movement have similarly worked against those on low income. Indeed the trade unions are being transformed almost out of recognition. Unlike previously, the main weight of membership now lies with some of the highest paid workers. The numbers of workers in trade unions fell from 53 per cent of the workforce in the late 1970s to 37 per cent eleven years later in 1990. Within this hardcore group of trade unionists the composition has changed very significantly. Union density is higher now amongst foremen and supervisors (46 per cent) than among workers with no managerial or supervisory responsibilities (37 per cent). Not surprisingly, union density is now highest amongst those with degree or equivalent qualifications (43 per cent) compared to those who have no qualifications at all (36 per cent). The current *Labour Force Survey* reveals that 53 per cent of union members hold non-manual jobs. Similarly, 44 per cent of union members worked in manufacturing in 1948 compared with only 24 per cent in 1991. In place of manufacturing, union strongholds are now to be found amongst public sector workers or those who were until recently classified as part of that group. In one of those strange ironies of history the trade union movement, if not fast becoming a bosses club, is certainly an alliance of managers and supervisors. It is very different from how it began as an organization to represent the interests of manual workers and poorer people.

On whatever grounds one chooses, the lot of the poor has deteriorated since 1979. Their numbers have increased two- to threefold. The gap between their income and that of other groups in the community has widened at a record rate. The picture is similar if living standards are considered. Indeed on one measurement the standard of living of the poorest 10 per cent of households has fallen by 6 per cent over the 1979 to 1989 decade. The richest 10 per cent gained at the same time an increase approaching 50 per cent.

It is widely assumed in political debate that with income tax benefiting all groups, even though the very richest gain more than the lion's share, with rocketing home ownership, the aspiring, successful sections of the population have been bonded together in a natural Conservative alliance – the top two-thirds of Great Britain against the rest.

It is true that unless Labour makes a number of key radical changes that alliance is likely to remain in place. But how firm is the cement? Where are the fault lines? Can the coalition be recast, including the poor, into a winning alliance?

Take home ownership. The advantage of owning one's own house remains considerable, despite falling asset prices and the slow turnover in the market. The down side comes in the size of mortgage debt. In the crazy atmosphere of the 1980s building societies inundated customers with offers to borrow more and more money. These extended mortgages were rarely spent on improving the property. Most were used for the purchase of other capital goods connected with the home. Mortgage debt presently stands at over £50 billion. For homes with mortgages this represents 54 per cent of their value – an unprecedented level. Spread over the population as a whole this means on average that the British carry £75 of mortgage debt for every £100 of net household income. Even by international standards this burden is unique and represents a major drag on a consumer-led recovery.

Debt is one issue which divides what might otherwise appear to be a homogeneous group. Another and more significant factor is income. The picture presented by commentators of changes in the 1980s is that the poor have been left behind in some no man's land. It is also asserted that the remains of what is left of the working class are ghettoed from the rest of Great Britain.

The facts simply do not bear out this description. Data from *Households Below Average Income* show not the egg-shaped income distribution described by commentators but rather an onion-shaped one. Two-thirds of the entire population live in households with incomes below the average. That fact has yet to be seized upon politically. *Two-thirds of the entire population live on incomes below the average*. There have been big changes in the size of income during the 1980s when, overall, living standards rose by

30 per cent. It is not, however, the case that society has left behind the poor and the remains of the working class. It is, rather, that the very, very rich, have drawn still further away from the rest of us.

The New Shape of British Society

Consider the percentage share of total original, gross disposable and post-tax income. On original income only the top 20 per cent show a gain in the proportion of total income: up from 43 per cent in 1979 to 49 per cent in 1989. Gross income shows the same trend. The only gain is by the richest 20 per cent, moving up from 37 per cent to 42 per cent of the total. Similarly, it is the top 20 per cent who are the only gainers if the measurement is disposable income, which has risen from 36 per cent to 41 per cent. And lastly, it is only the richest 20 per cent who mark up an increased share of post-tax income: from 37 per cent to 43 per cent. Much more data could be given taking different groupings, but each source without exception shows that while money and real incomes have increased, the bottom 80 per cent during the current spell of Conservative government have not increased their share of total income, no matter what measurement is taken. The top 20 per cent have.

The income data, especially the Government's *Households Below Average Income*, show that the poor are not a rigidly segregated group beneath the rest of us. We all know where they are in the income pile, but the definition of low income or poverty is inevitably arbitrary. Move the line just a little, and another huge army joins their ranks.

Let me return to Jan Pen's illustration of the inequality of income. This time let us imagine that people are lined up according to their income with the poor, for once, at the front of the queue and the rich at the back. The exercise is not to point to the differences between the top and the bottom of the income pile. Rather it is to show how bunched the distribution of income is. This time round people are asked to cross the line at exactly the same time as others cross who possess the same level of income.

As the hour clock starts people pass in front of us in large groups according to their shared incomes. In this march past, half of the entire population have passed the line within the first sixteen minutes. Two-thirds of the entire population have crossed over within 20 minutes. Three-quarters of the population have crossed within the first half an hour. That gives the reader some idea of where most of the voting population rank in respect of income.

Labour's Last Hope

The next stage in my argument is particularly crucial. I do not conclude from these figures that Labour has got it made. Neither have I ever begun, nor do I begin now, to peddle the view that it is all the fault of the voters. As soon as the Labour Party wakes up to the significance of these figures, and pitches its electoral tent accordingly, the Party will be able to link in the cause of the least privileged with the much wider group of voters.

It is the Party and not the voters who have got to wake up. The overwhelming majority of voters who cross the march past point within the first half an hour do identify a common interest, share many common aspirations, yet most of them do not think the Labour Party understands their lives to any significant degree. In a choice between no loaf and half a loaf, the majority consistently and understandably chooses half a loaf and votes Conservative. Labour's job is to present an alternative encompassing the whole loaf.

How this might be achieved is a huge exercise, but some of the directions that need to be taken are given in the following chapters. Unemployment is the key economic home issue and one to which the Tory Party reacts like a frightened rabbit. It is the key economic issue because of what it means to those who are condemned to idleness and a feeling of worthlessness as the rest of us in society go on our way earning a living. It is the key issue because at some stage Britain, and with it Europe, will disintegrate into social chaos and violence unless counter economic action is taken. It is the key economic issue because of the cost of the current dole queue. In evidence recently put before the Employment Select Committee, Gillian Shephard, the Employment Secretary, suggested that the cost to the taxpayer of extra benefits, the loss of income tax and the loss of indirect taxes averaged out at £9000 for each unemployed person. This is equivalent to some £900 million for every 100,000 people who are unemployed. Since three million people are unemployed the actual bill is in the region of £27 billion. It is the key economic issue because of the loss of economic growth which results from unemployment. The innovation of the Organization for Economic Co-operation and Development for measuring the severity of a recession is to calculate the potential output of an economy and examine the actual performance against that target. In 1982 the gap between potential and actual performance was estimated at 3.6 per cent. The latest OECD estimate is of a gap of 6.9 per cent and rising. Peter Kellner has estimated that in cash terms we are talking about a penalty in lost wealth of £55 billion a year – or £20 a week or £1000 a year for every single person. It does not take much imagination to consider what could be done with a sum of this dimension.

Politically, unemployment is important in another respect. Unemployment is much more evenly spread over the country during the current recession. This time the South has not been immune. It has also affected white- as well as blue-collar workers; far more of the population is affected by unemployment than at any other time during our generation. (Don't forget the million the Tories have wiped off the official role.) Families all over the country now have direct experience of some member being made unemployed, or of a school or college leaver being unable to find work. And because the total keeps rising there is a *fear* of unemployment which was not present before. No matter how much extra money is going into people's pockets – the cut in interest rates over the past 16 months resulted in a £30,000 mortgage holder gaining an extra £1,488 increase in income a year – consumers will not spend on the scale expected. Too many people believe that their shoulder may be the next one tapped by the unemployment recruiting officer.

Unemployment's dark shadow is falling on a larger and larger proportion of the population. A coherent and well-argued policy at home to move the country and Europe back towards full employment will be highly attractive. And here is the rub. Unemployment is also the greatest recruiting serjeant for poverty. Who said the interests of mainland Great Britain and the poor could not be aligned?

A similar initiative awaits the party on the welfare front. Here, in contrast to Labour's hesitancy, the Tory Party is moving swiftly behind the scene showing all its traditional certainty. In chapter five I propose that the half of British industry already theoretically owned by us through our pension funds, should actually be owned by each of us. Here I wish to stress that this transfer of over £250 billion of corporately held wealth to individuals will not cost the taxpayers a single penny. In that chapter I will again stress that the redistribution of pension funds is not a reform which necessarily means increasing taxes – indeed I will be talking about ways of cutting taxes – but a means of spreading success.

It was Siegfried Sassoon, I believe, who wrote, after meeting the working class in World War One's trenches, that if the English were promoted from inferno to paradise they would still gather around and talk about the less good old days. Taking a pleasure in failure is one of the least attractive sides of our national character.

Naturally Labour shares this national characteristic. Consequently, in welfare we see success purely in terms of increasing the size of the budget. We ought to be equally interested in seeing it reduced, but only as more and more of our fellow citizens have an adequate income from work and wealth or both.

One of our pressing concerns should be to see how the success of occupational pensions – and they have been the unsung success of the post-war period – can be spread to a greater number of individuals. If that is achieved fewer and fewer people will be at risk of poverty in old age. One aim of Labour's welfare policy must be to cut off the supply routes to deprivation.

No one can claim that this objective will not be in the interest of the poor, and will not be electorally popular, and will not cost the taxpayers a penny. In turn Labour will cease to be seen as being the party running an ambulance service, picking up capitalism's failures, and become perceived as the party concerned with spreading the success of industrialism to an increasing number of people.

Conclusion

One morning in September 1916 the news came that the economist Barbara Wootton's brother was reported missing. It was as a result of this tragedy that she first became aware of how the human mind tries to escape from an unbearable reality by concentrating on a totally insignificant point. Her brother had held the rank of Acting Captain. All the correspondence which her mother received from the War Office referred to him as a Lieutenant. Each time the post arrived Barbara's mother would suffer a fresh outbreak of intense indignation as if her grief was somehow deflected into the irritation caused by this inaccuracy. A year later when Barbara received a telegram telling her that her husband of a few weeks' standing had been killed the same psychological process was at work causing her to be constantly obsessed by the fact that one corner of the telegram was missing. As with humans so too with political parties. The horror of defeat four times over is too much to bear. Since the votes were counted in 1992 much of the Labour Party has been on autopilot, going through the motions of being an Opposition as a means of keeping at bay the great truth about the Tory election successes in the belief that next time the election pendulum will swing back.

At the heart of this response is a fear too awful for Labour even to voice. It is that the Tory's policy of redistribution of wealth has wrought a new agenda for which most of the cards are held by the voters and that they will continue to play them the Tories' way. But at the heart of this redistribution lies Labour's opportunity. Massive as the redistribution has been, it has left two-thirds of the electorate with incomes below the average. Here is the basis of a new coalition for radicals. Success here not only requires implementing the reforms advocated in the first chapter, but policies which, by working with the grain of human nature, are ones which instinctively appeal to the electorate. The remainder of the book examines such policies which, while remaining true to Labour's traditional ideals, attempt also to join hands with the future.

CHAPTER THREE

The Emergence of Britain's Underclass

One of the very real worries of Labour's traditionalists is that in developing a programme in tune with a majority of voters' aspirations, the Party will jettison its traditional beliefs in defending the interests of the poor and the underdog. One consequence of Mrs Thatcher's policies has been the emergence of an underclass in Britain. The presence of this new group not only challenges the Party but also offers it an opportunity. The challenge is to cut off the supply routes to the underclass while at the same time helping those who are already destitute. The task is to do so in a way which not only accords with the sympathies of many voters, but also offers opportunities to many of them as well.

Privileges Not Rights

At the outset it is important to explain how an essential part of British political society has operated over the past three hundred years or so. The conventional means of describing one of the crucial movements to shape our current society is to talk in terms of the rights of citizenship. These are generally divided into three dimensions: civil citizenship gained by equal rights before the courts, largely established during the eighteenth century, political rights or equal rights at the ballot box brought about by the extension of the franchise in the nineteenth century, and the gaining of social or economic rights during much of this century.

It matters little for the present task that these three moves do not fit precisely into the different centuries to which they are here allotted. What is important is that the whole debate about citizenship is mistaken, if not misleading. It is essentially a foreign way of trying to describe our political culture. The French mode, taking root as it did in the violence of the Revolution of 1789, is unknown in this country. Nobody talks about, goes on strike for, organizes marches around their rights to citizenship. The objection is not only that we don't think in such terms, and that such political language is therefore inappropriate, but that such language gives a totally misleading representation of how rights, or more accurately, how privileges operate within our own political system. The system of privileges, rather than of rights, is not a matter of mere semantics. Rights conjure up advances made from below, and are universally enforced. By contrast, the British process has been one of the élite's privileges shared, often under duress, with a wider group.

British Society's Cart of Privilege

Rather than seeing British society organized in such a way as to convey universal rights, a more accurate description of what happens in practice is to see government in terms of a cart transporting society's most valuable privileges. At times the cart slows down enough to allow more of the population to climb aboard and thus start the process of sharing society's privileges in a new way.

There is nothing clean, neat or tidy about the slowing down of the cart. A number of attempts were needed to ensure that all adult members of the population gained the right to vote. Neither were the times when groups climbed aboard well-planned events. The Campbell-Bannerman and Asquith Governments were radical by any definition, yet the Liberal manifesto for the 1906 election gave no hint of what was in store for the most privileged sections of the British establishment. Indeed the attempts to ward off the boarding parties during the stewardship of these Governments were more violent than at any other time during the past two hundred years.

In 1906, 1945 and again in 1979 boarding parties were successful in joining their more privileged countrymen. The 1906 Liberal Government began the process of extending income security to the elderly, the sick and the unemployed – a large group of voters. The 1945 Government was more ambitious. The vast majority of the population gained the privilege of being lifted free from poverty as the Government gave the insurance schemes almost universal cover. The cart again slowed in 1979 and in so doing allowed huge armies of people to gain the privileges of owning their own homes.

Nineteen seventy-nine is notable for another reason. It was the first known instance of groups being simultaneously thrown off the cart, stripped of their privileges and left largely to fend for themselves. It is part of this 'throwing off' process that I see as bringing about the growth of an underclass. Despite the way this term has been used by right-wing popular writers and politicians, it is a useful tool both to highlight a new and disturbing contemporary trend, and to show the meaning of a phrase can be developed to meet current ideological demands.

Constructing an Underclass

The term 'underclass' was first used by Swedish economist Gunnar Myrdal. Writing in the early 1960s he used it to describe the effects of long-term unemployment on the ability of individuals to re-enter the workforce. In Myrdal's opinion long-term unemployment created an underclass of

> unemployed and, gradually, unemployable persons and families at the bottom of society in which, for the majority of people above that level, the increasingly democratic structures of the educational system creates more and more liberty – real liberty – and equality of opportunity.

It is important to pause and consider the implication of Myrdal's views. He gave equal emphasis to the cause of the underclass – unemployment – and the psychological effect it had on its victims. But Myrdal's comprehension of the issue was such that both Left and Right came to distance themselves from him – the Left because he was prepared to consider the personal psychological damage unemployment inflicts upon individuals, and the Right because of the equal stress he gave to unemployment's structural causes.

Myrdal was of course right to stress both the structural and psychological aspects. If the Right is blind in its left eye in not seeing the structural causes, the Left is equally blind in its right eye in being unable to see that a major part of the political anger about unemployment should come from its deadly effect on individuals.

From such beginnings the term has been largely refashioned, from one that is intended to describe the causes of a predicament, together with its consequences, to a means of blaming the victim. In America the underclass is now defined in terms of lawless young blacks and black single-mothers. And the reason for this redefinition? Irony upon irony, the underclass has been nurtured by the very programme that was created to counter it. Welfare payments act like fortified baby milk. Under such care the problem doesn't wither away. It grows ever more strong and powerful. No prizes for guessing that this view became common currency as Republicans demanded cuts in welfare as the principal means of reducing taxes.

Poverty During Full Employment

Let me return to the British scene and examine the circumstances prior to many people's expulsion from privileges in the 1980s to which I have already referred. The background is a period of full employment. Although British society polarized along class lines, there is a general agreement that, during the initial postwar period of full employment, a bi-partisan political approach operated to prevent an exacerbation of these class differences.

Now let us consider what happened to class differences during this period. I present four snap-shots, each suggesting how vulnerable the poorest were even during this most favoured period.

The first snap-shot comes from data on infant mortality. Because very young babies are so vulnerable, their survival can be affected by social and economic conditions. Indeed their vulnerability is such that they often register societal changes before other groups. Since the war there have been three bench-mark studies of children born during specific weeks. The initial work that resulted in longitudinal studies was carried out in 1946, 1958 and in 1970. Over this time span significant improvements took place in the health of mothers and babies. The number of babies dying during the initial stages of life showed a sharp fall. Yet this dramatic decline in the number of infant deaths was not accompanied by a similar narrowing of class mortality differences. Once the dead infants recorded in the 1970 study were classified by the occupation of their fathers it was found that 'the striking feature . . . apart from the high perinatal rate of unsupported mothers . . . is the persisting steep social class gradient in mortality.'

No further national bench-mark surveys have been carried out. Since 1975, however, data have been produced which allow the period up to 1979 to be considered. Whatever measure is taken – still births, deaths during the first week of life, or at any time during the first year – the resulting picture shows major class differences in survival. The largest class difference in survival was, in fact, registered once babies had left hospital, were back home and were exposed to different living standards. The death rate amongst the poorest babies after the first month of life was exactly twice that of babies from richer homes.

The second snap-shot of vulnerability comes from the performance of the poorest children at school. As with the survival chances of babies from different social backgrounds, the evidence points to persisting differences along class lines in school performance. A special study was made of the poorest children born during a single week in 1958. It is important to stress that we are reporting on the welfare of children born into full employment Britain, and yet the home backgrounds of these children presented major obstacles to educational advance.

The most disadvantaged children were likely not only to share a bedroom, but also to share a bed. Some of these children both shared and were still wetting their bed at the age of eleven, or shared a bed with a brother or sister who wet the bed. It requires little imagination to register the disturbed sleep and the cross-infection to which many disadvantaged children were therefore exposed, or the condition of many of these children when they appeared at school. Nor is it surprising that, when these vulnerable children were tested, they generally recorded ability levels well below those of other children.

What happens at school provided the background for the third snap-shot of vulnerability. Here we focus on school leavers' attempts to enter the labour market during Britain's most prosperous years. In the early post-war years the vast majority of working-class children left school at fifteen and few had any qualifications to present to their potential employers. They didn't need qualifications for the jobs in which they would be employed for the rest of their working lives. The very brightest working-class children, of course, won scholarships to grammar schools and most of this group left school with qualifications and took up places in what is called the expanding salariat.

Until fairly recently, therefore, the crucial question for parents and politicians centred on the role schools played in determining which pupils rose socially. Gaining a grammar school place was crucial if working-class children were to gain a place in the salariat. With the rise in the school leaving age to sixteen, the number of pupils leaving school with some qualifications increased substantially. These qualifications not only decide who gets a successful career in the salariat of post-war Britain, but who, by being part of a minority without qualifications (instead of what was once the majority) is most likely to face greatest difficulty in finding a job. These changes mean that the attention focuses less on selection of secondary schools (the majority of them now operate as comprehensives) than on selection and entry to the labour market. Here the crucial question concerns the qualifications the entrants bring with them. It is hardly surprising to learn that those children who had most difficulty in surviving birth, who also share beds, have disturbed sleep, who are most prone to illness and school absences, are overwhelmingly, although not exclusively, to be found in the ranks of the unskilled, unqualified school leaver. Although at a distinct disadvantage in the kind of jobs they obtained, these children nevertheless did gain jobs.

Consider what happens now. The labour market for young people has shrunk, with many of them left unemployed and unemployable, watching as their more qualified peers are carried away on the economic tide to varying degrees of economic success.

One last snap-shot. The labour market into which these children went to find work was also changing over and above the newfound thirst for qualifications. Perhaps the post-war status quo was an aberration. Or perhaps memories play tricks with all of us. Or perhaps the image of a job for life in a single firm was simply a very inaccurate picture of what life was actually like. Whatever the truth, current trends, which are euphemistically seen as spreading 'greater flexibility', are having a profound effect on the life of the poorest. There has, for example, been a mushrooming of part-time jobs, doubling to over four million in the two decades up to 1981, while full-time employment fell by two million over the same period. That trend continued, though at a slightly less rapid rate, during the 1980s.

Part-time work is often presented with a missionary zeal as

fulfilling a legitimate demand of an increasing proportion of the workforce. While no one wishes to dispute the claim that women in particular look for work patterns which fit in with their home responsibilities, and that more men in future may make similar demands, the argument nonetheless distorts the real debate that is going on in the country. There are simply millions of people who wish to work full-time, but take part-time work because that is all that is on offer. It is an error of gigantic proportions to then deduce from the figures that, because part-time jobs or temporary jobs are hurriedly filled, that is what is really demanded.

There has also been a dramatic rise in the number of people working on a temporary basis. Temporary work divides into seasonal, temporary or casual work on the one hand, and, on the other, work contracted for a fixed period of time. Agency and professional workers are to be found in this second category. When temporary workers were asked to classify themselves, two-thirds placed themselves in the first category. While a higher proportion of temporary workers are women workers, temporary workers are also considerably younger than most workers, largely because a higher proportion of them are still teenagers. A staggering one in five were under twenty years old, and a quarter of all teenage workers in the labour force work on a temporary basis. Many of these young people would be occupying relatively low-skilled positions and receive little or no training.

The Rise of the Youthful Underclass

The difficulties of surviving birth, of home conditions which put up barriers to getting the most out of school, a labour market which is demanding greater skilled qualifications from the majority of the workforce, while producing secondary, often part-time work for other unskilled workers, are all part of the realities of the life faced by a growing number of young people. These trends were clearly apparent during the post-war boom, although, of course, they became more and more pronounced as the boom conditions gradually gave way to the rising unemployment of the 1980s and the slump of the 1990s. It is against this background that we need to consider Mrs Thatcher's policies of attempting to instil greater responsibility into the lives of poorer families. Once these two separate pieces of information are brought together – the longer term trends that force a growing number of young people to the very margins of working life, and the series of doses of medicine from Mrs Thatcher's bottle labelled 'Parental Responsibility' – we can begin to explain why Britain has an emerging underclass of young people.

Let us begin by examining the state of play in 1979 before reviewing the measures that Mrs Thatcher's governments took to enhance family responsibility for their offspring. In that year, of all sixteen to eighteen year olds 28 per cent of them remained in full-time education, and an even greater percentage, 63 per cent, were in work, while of the remainder, 3 per cent were in training and 6 per cent were registered as unemployed. Ten years later 73 per cent were in full-time education, 14 per cent in training and 3 per cent were officially registered as unemployed. But even the decline of the numbers employed to 46 per cent concealed the full extent of the declining job opportunities for sixteen to eighteen year olds.

A twin policy was adopted to reduce or restrict the right to benefit of young people while at the same time increasing the number of training places so that, finally, in 1988 training became compulsory for young unemployed people. The first restriction or cut in a young person's right to benefit came in November 1980 when supplementary benefit for school leavers was deferred until the start of the new academic year. Half a million young people lost income by this move. In 1983 and 1984 the housing benefit paid to young people to pass onto their parents with whom they were living was abolished, first for sixteen year olds, then the restriction was extended to seventeen year olds and finally to all eighteen to twenty year olds. As a consequence, 460,000 families lost benefit. A further cut in the payment towards rent was made in 1984 when the amounts that young people were supposed to contribute towards this payment was raised. By 1988, when the age of claiming benefit was raised officially from sixteen to eighteen years (the first time such a change had been made since 1948), benefits for young people had already been cut on fourteen separate occasions.

In theory, each of these moves should have spirited a greater bonding between parents and their offspring. But let's consider the reality. Parents on low income often express to me their profound sense of failing their children – 'failing' is the very word they use. During so much of the time that they have spent raising their children they have said 'no' to requests which they know the children of other, better-off families, have been granted. To say young people in their late adolescent years are anxious to get onto a par for the first time with their peers in terms of dress and lifestyle is to underestimate the force of this wish. The Thatcher Government changed the rules so that the parents' social security claim is calculated on the assumption that generous payments are being made by their offspring to household costs. Not to claim this money pushes the family into rent arrears and into other debts. To claim the money is to crush the young person's urge to make up for past, hard times. The outcome for all too many poor families is not to foster greater bonding but indeed the opposite.

Now add to this heady mixture the parallel changes in what the dry, official language calls board and lodging payments. In 1983 young people under seventeen became ineligible for these payments if they stayed within their local area. Single unemployed people under twenty-five were only able to claim benefit outside their locality and then for only two, four or eight weeks, depending upon where they claimed. After this time limit they would have to move to another area if they wished to continue claiming benefit. Thus began the drive to push people out of their own home localities into a nomadic lifestyle.

The Reappearance of the Young Homeless

Changes in social security made it more difficult for young people to stay at home. Simultaneously, social security changes were made to make it much more difficult for young people to 'board out', even though many of these young people had previously been in local authority care and had no 'home' to go to. Here then is the pincer movement which goes a long way to explaining why so many young people sleep rough each night on the streets of our major cities, and why they are a morëcommon sight on city streets than are police men and women. And, as if the rules have been designed to keep people homeless once they hit rock-bottom, the Government have abolished advance payments for rent. Up until 1988 the claimants finding lodgings were able to offer landlords advance rent which came as part of their benefit. When this was abolished many landlords were not prepared to take the risk of having claimants on social security who might not regularly pay their rent. This is even more true of those landlords who require deposits as well as rent payments.

That the payment of advance rents could prevent many people from being homeless was born out by a local project in Birkenhead. The churches run a night-shelter each year during the worst winter months. Called The Ark, this project in the Wirral highlights how homelessness is endemic amongst young people in all areas of the country, not just in London and other major cities. Two years ago the Transport and General Workers' Union ran a night-shelter in the dock area of Birkenhead. It looked after a total of seventy-five people – mainly young men – during its seven weeks of operation. Last year and this the churches ran The Ark project out of two premises in Wallasey, a more prosperous area. A different group of homeless people presented itself made up far more evenly of old and young men.

In 1992, 136 people lived in The Ark. The youngest was sixteen; the oldest was seventy-two. Homeless people dismissed from hospital were sent to the Ark. Phil, one of the younger residents, described how he had slept on the floor of numerous friends' homes before becoming permanently homeless. Prior to his six weeks in The Ark he had been sleeping in the sheds on a local allotment site. He knew he was trespassing, knew he could be punished, but found it a risk worth taking in order to get some shelter during the coldest part of the winter. Phil's predicament illustrates the extent of the hidden homelessness amongst young people, the armies who sleep on the floor of friends for a few nights before moving off to another vacant floor. All the residents at The Ark were local people.

Homelessness has also come as a result of many young people moving to major cities in search of work. Having no job means depending on benefits. No advance payments for rent result directly in homelessness for many young people. One in five of all twenty-five year olds is officially registered as unemployed. It is anyone's guess what the true level of homelessness is. Homelessness compounds the victim's vulnerability and breaks the link between electors and the elected. It almost invariably means losing the vote. So the group most damaged by government policy has no legitimate voice with which to strike back or express its grievance.

Disenfranchising the Young and Vulnerable

I now use the term 'underclass' to mark this totally new development in Britain where large numbers of people have been pushed off the metaphorical cart and stripped of their privileges. Never before in this century has such a process occurred. Indeed, up until 1979, this century is marked by the very opposite trend of extending social security cover. Since Mrs Thatcher's first election win a whole series of moves has disenfranchised groups of predominantly young and vulnerable people from receiving social security. When one looks at the home background of many of these young

71

people, or indeed the lack of any home background for a sizeable proportion of them, the withdrawal of board and lodging cover for people who stay in their own home town, the loss of being able to make advance rent payments for lodgings, the wonder is not that there are so many young people sleeping rough on the city streets, but that there aren't a great deal more.

I have dwelt at length with the desperate plight of the young single homeless because they are by far and away the largest group within Britain's underclass. What can possibly go on in the heads of the thousands upon thousands of young people who sleep in shop doorways, in the entrances into major buildings, under bridges and similar places each night? With such an army of dispossessed the question is not why are there so many crimes committed in inner-city areas; it is, rather, why aren't there more? It says something extraordinary about the English character that these armies of young people sit peacefully to beg. They similarly make extraordinary attempts to keep clean. They queue quietly in supermarkets to get their sliced white bread and margarine and then walk peacefully away. Some drink. It is amazing that they don't all want to stay drunk all of the time. It is equally amazing that most of us shuffle past them in embarrassment. Last winter I slept out for a single night for a fund-raising effort along with other MPs. Sleeping out only once, and knowing that it would never occur again, and doing so with friends, was nonetheless a salutary experience. For one night no address, no contact point, no post, no phone, no shelter. For a whole lifetime? No refuge, no family, no doctor, no work, no hope. The list of deprivations is almost endless.

We have to ask why there are hordes sleeping rough. Has there been a sudden collapse of character since 1979? Or is the disgraceful spectacle on our streets brought about by a lethal combination of record unemployment and social security cuts which have forced people away from their homes and their neighbourhoods where they have family and friends?

Action for Today and Policies for Tomorrow

Reforms need to be thought of in three stages – the cart has to be slowed down on three separate occasions in order to get back on board those ruthlessly pushed off since 1979. There are those immediate actions which offer individuals a chance of moving off the streets and into reasonable accommodation. Next is a whole raft of policies aimed at preventing young people from being expelled from their own homes and neighbourhoods. The last tranche of policies aims at knitting the underclass back into mainstream society. In doing so the interests of a much wider group of voters are also clearly being simultaneously served.

First, in constructing the immediate exits from the underclass, two moves are urgent. Advance payments for rent together with a scheme of deposits where these are demanded by landlords must be reintroduced. As I have already mentioned, workers at The Ark in Birkenhead could find lodgings for each homeless person presenting themselves at the project if advance rent payments and deposits could be given to the landlords. No such advance payments are forthcoming from social security. A pilot scheme making such advance rent payments is being run in London. The Government refuses to extend the scheme until the research on this pilot project is complete. In the interim homeless people remain on the streets.

There are no obvious reasons why this system of payment was abolished in the first place. The official line is that the advance payments end up in the pockets of the claimants or the landlord whenever the former has to move to a new address. This excuse cannot be left unchallenged. It cannot be beyond the wit of officialdom to keep accurate accounts so that those who gain advance payments and deposits are not paid their rent allowance during the last two weeks of their stay (or whatever time the advance payments cover) in any particular accommodation.

Second, once these payments are in existence, voluntary

organizations need to be alerted not only to changes in the rules, but in the scope for finding homeless young people good lodgings. Indeed, once the word gets about that the rules have been changed some young people themselves will find their own accommodation. Others who have been on the streets for some time, and have no possessions apart from what they carry around all the time, will probably need some half-way stop before successfully gaining lodgings. Those voluntary groups working with young homeless people will need extra financial support to provide this bridge back into ordinary society.

These are the two most immediate and simple moves which would allow young, single, homeless people to get back on the cart and begin again to share the basic privilege of having a roof over their heads. At the same time steps must be made to stop pushing other young people off the cart which contains society's main privileges. Measures need to be taken to cut off the supply routes into the underclass.

The justification for raising eligibility for income support from sixteen to eighteen years was the Government's pledge that all young people in this age group would be in full-time education, in work, or on a youth training scheme. All YTS recruits are given an allowance of £29.50 if they are seventeen and £35 if they are a year older – sums which have not changed since the mid-1980s. The Government promised that training places would be available for all sixteen to eighteen year olds wanting such a course. The pledge then went through what can only be described as a laundry operation. Courses would be available but they might not be immediately on offer. Or they might be on immediate offer, but not in the areas in which the young person lived – as though course vacancies in Blackburn were relevant to young people living fifty miles away in Birkenhead. More recently the Government has admitted that course places might not be immediately available, but it hasn't adapted the rules to take into account this most basic of admissions.

Those unable to gain a YTS place may make an application

for what is called a special hardship payment. To do so young people must register at the careers' office and take proof of their registration to the Unemployment Benefit office. The Unemployment Benefit office will then issue the young person with a form to take to the Benefit Agency office, where he or she will be interviewed. The Benefit Agency office will then submit a claim to what is called the Special Hardship Claims Unit who will have to make a decision within twenty-four hours. Payments for successful applicants are, however, paid one to two weeks in arrears, so young people needing money urgently have to make a claim to the Social Fund for a crisis loan. The Special Hardship Claims Unit makes a decision as to whether benefits should be paid. But it is the adjudicating officer at the local Benefit Agency office who decides how income support should be paid and whether a claim is granted. There are no clear, let alone binding guidelines as to who can qualify for social hardship payments. This is the procedure for youngsters, many of whom are on the brink of destitution. And the procedure is one instituted by a government which boasts of its mission to cut out the red tape and simplify the bureaucratic system.

There is evidence of the extent to which the Government exposes legions of young people to near or actual destitution and, often, homelessness. Youthaid estimates from official figures that almost 125,000 young people are unemployed and almost three quarters of this group gain no official financial help whatsoever. A MORI poll found that 45 per cent of those claiming special hardship payments had slept rough, but MORI could only poll those who were getting some help and claiming benefit. The extent of homelessness amongst those groups who fail to make their way through the bureaucratic maze erected by the Government is obviously impossible to determine, but homelessness and destitution amongst the 90 per cent who gain no benefit whatsoever must be the norm.

Reforms are urgent. The first is to ensure that guaranteed places are available for those young people seeking training.

The first time many of them in their adult life come into contact with the Government is when they seek their guaranteed training place. How will these young people regard officialdom in the future if on their first brush with it they find the word 'guarantee' when used by the Government means something very different to what most of us would have thought it meant? That a quarter of young people seeking a guaranteed place fail to find one speaks for itself.

Given the Government's inability to deliver its own promise, a full training allowance should be paid to all applicants for courses rather than those who are lucky enough to gain a place. Next, housing grants given to local authorities and housing associations need to reflect more accurately the changing composition of households, taking into consideration the growing number of people living alone which now accounts for over a quarter of all households.

Third, much more attention needs to be given to young people leaving care and establishing a home of their own. All homeless surveys point to the vulnerability of this group. The Barnardo's Tyneside project reports one person they helped telling them that 'on my sixteenth birthday I moved from a children's home to a bedsit. I did not know how to turn a cooker on even.' A National Childrens' Home project in Scotland cited the example of a sixteen-year-old girl leaving care who had been homeless for three weeks. During that time this young person had no money and was in receipt of no benefit. No child should be allowed to leave care at sixteen unless they want to, and then only if they have a job or a YTS place. All of these young people should also be offered a guarantee of foster parents if they do not wish immediately to set up in a bedsit on their own. Each of them should also know that if they face difficulties they would be welcome back at the children's home. Social services departments must keep regular contact with each child leaving care, and each young person should know which person in the social services department is responsible for keeping in touch with them.

These reforms aim to improve immediately the lot of the underclass and to do so with the support of those who share a sense of shame that a British government edict has given birth to an underclass in Britain. Moral outrage is still, thankfully, a basis upon which to help galvanize a winning coalition of votes. But longer term reforms are also required. And here Labour has an opportunity of linking the needs of the most vulnerable young people to a much wider appeal.

Reference only needs to be made here to two proposals that are developed later. The backdrop to every young person sleeping rough on the streets is the persistence of large numbers of people who have been without work year in and year out. While the level of unemployment began to rise appreciably in the middle to late 1960s the current, persistent long-term unemployment is a phenomenon established during the 1980s. All the razzmatazz surrounding attempts about jump-starting the British economy into a higher rate of economic growth blinded us to what was happening to the length of time people were required to stand in the dole queue. Chapter Four and the final chapter look at how a programme to help the immediate long-term unemployed should be built into a total economic package aimed at full employment.

Tax reforms are also relevant to the issues considered in this section. A crucial objective of the Labour Party should be to reduce substantially the standard rate of tax, not merely to the Tory target of 20p in the pound, but to a target rate of 15p. This in itself could be achieved by abolishing existing tax relief for pensions and mortgage interest. The Left, sadly, still fails to appreciate the impact income tax has on the wage packets of lower paid workers. Practically all the jobs advertised in the Birkenhead job centre are appallingly low paid. And yet, appalling as these rates of pay are, National Insurance contributions, which commence at £56 for employees, and income tax of 20 per cent begin to bite into these meagre pay packets at £66 per week. The importance of tax reform in improving incentives and in safe-guarding already fragile living standards merely needs to be underlined at this point.

Educating a Workforce, not an Elite

One of the biggest dangers in using the term 'underclass' is that it gives the impression of a simple social problem whose causes are easy to understand and address. This, however, is not the case. The reforms must reflect this complexity and extend beyond the payment of social security benefits. If we are serious about reversing the growth of an underclass, we must confront the institutions that produce young people who are so vulnerable that changes in the benefit rules alone can force them into destitution. For this reason the third long-term reform must be concerned with the poor performance of many of our secondary schools, since it is amongst those gaining least from eleven years of educational investment that the underclass is predominantly drawn. Here I am not making the criticisms so often heard of comprehensive schools failing to develop fully the abilities of their most gifted pupils. It is rather the failure of secondary schools to have a curriculum which is as attractive as it is valuable for those who are dubbed 'non-academic' children. This phrase is as condescending as it is misleading. The mind slips too easily from accepting some children as 'non-academic' to believing that they are thick or that there are no intellectual skills which aren't within the academic domain. Here are important issues which, by slight of language, are not faced.

I first realized that truancy was a far larger problem than education officials and experts would admit after observing during school hours the large number of young people drifting around the centre of Birkenhead. Apart from the numbers involved, I learnt two valuable pieces of information from these young people. First, although many of them admitted that it was pretty boring loafing about all day, or ganging up in one or other of their homes, such boredom was preferable to what was on offer at school. Second, once a pupil had become part of a truanting gang, considerable peer pressure is applied to prevent the gang dispersing and going back to school.

The universal complaint by the young truants is the senselessness and uselessness of most of what they are being taught in school. They can see little relevance in what they learn at school to what they optimistically hope to do when leaving school and seeking a job. Even allowing for the extent to which young people will tell a good yarn, particularly to their MP, this complaint needs to be addressed head-on.

The Government's customer orientated delivery of public services needs to be applied to schools. Its reform of the curriculum has in fact had more than a flavour of an old-fashioned élitist approach. A new syllabus built around the national curriculum, but offering B.Tec courses to pupils in their mid years of secondary education, is now urgent and overdue. The B.Tec qualifications are, as the name suggests, technically biased, and are built up on a modular basis. Pupils therefore quickly experience success, gain confidence from that success, and build on it. B.Tec courses are also attractive in that each major qualification is validated as being equal to other non-technical qualifications. B.Tec qualifications do not therefore ghetto students into a single line of education. They are qualifications which the students can see as relevant and applicable to their life after leaving school. Success not only builds up a student's confidence. B.Tec qualifications are inter-changeable with more traditional qualifications, and therefore keep open the possibilities for students to transfer to other types of courses later in their career should they so wish.

This reform needs to be set within much wider parameters, and parameters which appeal to voters who are as interested in the effectiveness of our educational system as they are in reforms for improving our country's economic performance.

A deep snobbishness infects English society, and one area

where this is most marked is in the élite's view of technical education. This stems from an equally perverse judgement that being in trade is of a lesser social standing than belonging to the professions, which is itself of a lower standing than doing nothing at all and living off unearned income. There is an in-built bias against a proper evaluation of technical education.

The Government, by establishing City Technology Colleges (CTCs), has made one major attempt to strike out in a sane direction. But the experiment has failed. While large numbers of children are acquiring first-class education in CTCs, the cost of these establishments prohibits their multiplication on a scale necessary to have an impact on the nature and tone of secondary education. The CTC experiments now need to be followed up by local authorities with the power to opt some of their secondary schools into a nationwide network of technical college schools. The aim should be to create a thousand technical college schools within the life of a parliament. Expansion on this scale would then overcome the other failure associated with CTCs, which is that because there are very few of these bodies they have themselves become élite-orientated, producing pupils many of whom will invariably move into pure rather than applied science at a degree stage. This country has always been able to produce fine pure scientists; what we are desperately short of is applied scientists to work as managers and foremen. A raft of a thousand technical college schools could do much to redress this long-standing weakness in British industry.

One last thought which relates to how these technical qualifications should be validated. And here another opportunity arises, if not of countering British snobbishness, of harnessing it to good effect. I have suggested elsewhere that the validation of technical and vocational qualifications should be brought together under the auspices of a Royal College. This was a view put forward by Prince Albert 140 years ago and could usefully be taken up by his great-great-great-grandson. Furthermore, there could be few better qualified people to give the right social cachet to this new validating procedure than the present Prince of Wales. The deep snobbery in British culture would then be mobilized to raise both the profile, accessibility, and attractiveness of technical and vocational education in this country. This change would then knit into the other long-term question of how best to raise the skills of Britain's labour force in a way that links with a recovery and rebuilding of our manufacturing base, all of which are issues considered in the final chapter.

Conclusion

One of the characteristics of British society for over two hundred years has been the way people have been incorporated into life's privileges. While the underclass has continued to grow since 1979, it has also been accompanied by an expulsion of a very vulnerable group from society's protection. Today, for the first time in two generations we see young beggars in an ever-growing number of urban areas. This British underclass is there because of the twin evils of unemployment and the withdrawal of social security cover. Further recruits for the underclass are being made ready by a secondary school curriculum which is perceived by many young people as useless in equipping them for life's work. It is by developing a new style of technical college school that the immediate needs of tomorrow's potential underclass can be met. The reform can also be knitted into a programme which builds up a wider coalition of parents who are concerned about the suitability of the education offered to their children in secondary schools. While this underclass is the most vulnerable in our society there are other groups too for which positive help is long overdue. To these people for whom exits from welfare are urgently needed we now turn.

CHAPTER FOUR

The Other Side of the UK

Once the French Impressionists gained a hold on the imagination of the public, other artists, once prized in the *salons*, soon fell out of favour. The technical value of their work had not changed. The value put on them half a century later by the buying public certainly did. Their work became condescendingly dismissed as belonging to the other side of the nineteenth century. Distance and barriers were erected and, as with pictures, so, sadly, with people. The same process can be seen to be at work much more generally in British society. This chapter looks at those people in our community who have been deemed by the wealthy, the privileged, the powerful, and sometimes not so powerful, to be on the other side of the United Kingdom.

Man-Made Differences

Qualities inherent in individuals do not vary that greatly. Differences between people there certainly are. But God-made differences between individuals are held within a fairly tight rein. A few people are three times cleverer than the least clever individual. Even fewer people are three times taller than the least tall adult. Now consider man-made differences. The highest paid command rewards hundreds and sometimes thousands more than that of the poorest paid. The same applies to the holding of wealth. The least privileged have almost no material wealth. The richest command riches beyond the dreams of avarice.

Most, but not all of the poorest depend upon welfare. As we

saw in Chapter Two, the numbers of people on welfare have grown inexorably: the increase in welfare recipients since the Tories won their first election victory in 1979 has been greater than the whole of the period since the establishment of the modern welfare state in 1948.

There has been an obvious corollary to this trend. The growing number on welfare has been accompanied by a similar explosion in expenditure. Forty-seven per cent of GDP is spent by the Government and by far the biggest slice of the Government budget goes on welfare. The cry is now up from the Government ranks that the welfare budget must be cut. The Treasury has instructed the three biggest spenders — social security, health and education — to consider what long-term restructuring (i.e., cuts) can take place in their budget.

Labour's Commission on Social Justice is giving its attention to the size and the distribution of the welfare budget. Its emphasis is likely to be on ways of more effectively spending the £90 billion welfare budget. But, as I have already suggested, Labour's approach needs to be much more radical. The aim should be to cut the welfare budget, but not, I hasten to add, in order to cut the rate of income tax, although this is an important objective. Nor should it be to bring down a Public Sector Borrowing Requirement which grows like Topsy, important as this will be once the economy begins to recover from the slump. Rather, cuts in welfare should be a sign of the success of Labour's strategy of providing a growing proportion of the population with work and wealth.

How can a programme be launched which will achieve this objective? Of course a strategy for full employment is more than a crucial ingredient. Without success on this front the task becomes near impossible. The failure to achieve full employment condemns millions to idleness and welfare dependency from which there are almost no exits. Work not only increases a person's income, and his or her share of the country's total income, but also the chance of acquiring a large stake in the country's wealth through membership of a pension scheme.

A second strategy needs simultaneously to be developed to cut off other supply routes to long-term welfare dependency. This approach needs to be followed by policies tailored to offer exits to those who find themselves locked into means-tested welfare. It is these people who are currently drawing welfare with no prospect of being freed who are the concern of this section. Three groups are the focal point of attention: the long-term unemployed, very young single mothers and the poorest pensioners. It is these groups who populate 'the other side' of Great Britain. First let us consider the situation of the poorest pensioners, where recent developments, far from cutting off the supply routes to poverty, are acting as recruiting sergeants for tomorrow's elderly poor.

Let me record two seemingly contradictory sets of information. The Government understandably likes quoting the importance of occupational pensions where, on average, the value is about equal to the state's flat-rate national insurance pension. But the majority of today's pensioners are still poor and many would consider them to be very poor. Sixty-one per cent of pensioner households have an income of under £5,000 a year. Overwhelmingly – but not exclusively – the oldest pensioners are also poorest. Twenty-nine per cent of pensioners with incomes below £5,000 are aged between seventy-five and seventy-nine. Twenty-two per cent are aged eighty or more. Those in the seventy to seventy-four year old bracket represent 17 per cent of those with incomes under £5,000 and a mere 7 per cent are sixty to sixty-four year olds – largely, no doubt, due to a combination of occupational pensions and income from work.

Yet the success in the occupational pension front is impressive – one of the unsung successes of the post-war period. Over half of all pensioners and two-thirds of recently retired pensioners receive an income from their occupational pension. Almost three-quarters of people in work are now members of occupational or personal pensions.

It is unlikely, however, that we are going to see any major increase in the numbers of members in what are called final salary schemes — i.e., a wage-related pension scheme where contributors hope to gain pensions of up to two-thirds of their final salary. Over the past decade the growth centre has shifted from final salary schemes to occupational money purchase and portable personal pensions. These are schemes which are not related to the size of a contributor's final salary but to the size of the contribution he or she has made during their working lives. Employers can and do make contributions to these schemes. In this latter category there has been an increase of six million members in less than ten years.

There is also another source of pension income which is important. In 1957 Labour published its proposals for a National Superannuation Scheme to run alongside the flat-rate old-age pension which would constitute a third and major component of pension income. The aim was that this pension should be pay related. The legislative effects of this policy were not to be seen until the 1966 parliament, but, as it was only introduced late into that parliament, the bill had not completed its passage when the 1970 election was called. The bill therefore failed to reach the statute book. A slim-line version of the measure was reintroduced in 1974 and became effective in 1978 under the name of the State Earnings Related Pension Scheme (SERPS). SERPS payments are an important source of income for a growing number of pensioners, and especially for the 70 per cent of newly retired men entitled to them. This sector of pension provision will also continue to play a growing part in the total income of pensioners. The total value of SERPS payments which stood at £800 million in 1990/1 will rise to £4 billion by the year 2000.

The aim of private pension schemes, and the fall-back cover of SERPS, was to ensure that a growing proportion of pensioners would be lifted free from poverty. However, a number of recent developments means that a growing number of pensioners may not have an adequate income in future years. Two changes are crucial. The 1983 Government seriously curtailed the scope of SERPS when cuts were made to the value of pensions, particularly to lower paid workers, to women generally and to widows. As well as making SERPS a less attractive proposition, members were also actively encouraged to opt out and make arrangements for themselves in the private sector. Such opting-out was envisaged in the 1957 proposals but only if the private schemes provided a more generous pension income. That safeguard, however, does not now apply.

Here then is the first cause for concern. In place of the certainty that, over time, a rising proportion of pensioners would gain an ever more generous pension from their occupational scheme, there is a growing uncertainty as to whether the private pension will be adequate to afford a minimum, let alone a generous retirement income. A decade ago the spread of occupational schemes appeared to have cut the supply route to poverty in old age. The pension reforms of the 1980s may have opened up a whole maze of routes back into this historic link.

Another of the major supply routes into poverty in old age is already apparent, and here lies the second cause for concern. Unemployment not only reduces a family's immediate income; its tentacles stretch way into the future affecting the retirement income of the unemployed person. Unemployment cuts off a person's membership of an occupational pension scheme. It also makes it impossible to continue membership of a privately arranged pension provision. The longer a person is unemployed the more likely the break in contributions and the greater the chance that what pension wealth has been built up will be realized at only a fraction of its true value. Today's slump is not only responsible for much of today's misery resulting from low income – it is also storing up similar misery in old age for the very people who are currently bearing society's unemployment. Radical reform of provision is called for on these grounds alone. But there are two further forces at work similarly demanding action.

The impact of the Thatcher Government's decision to break the uprating link for pensions between earnings or prices, taking whichever was the more favourable to pensioners, has almost escaped public comment. Yet here, at the heart of the state's provision for retired people, is a depth charge exploding with increasing force each year. At its peak, the state old-age pension was valued at over 30 per cent of average earnings for a married couple and 20 per cent for a single pensioner. The old-age pension currently stands at 25 per cent and 15 per cent of average earnings respectively for married and single pensioners. The Government blandly asserts that the value of pensions will remain at this level indefinitely. For that happy scenario to become a reality requires that earnings will rise at no greater rate than prices, an event unknown for any length of time during the last three hundred years. On the more realistic assumption that earnings will continue to outstrip prices, the relative value of the state pension as measured against average earnings will continue to fall as the pensions are upgraded in line with prices only. The Institute of Fiscal Studies calculated that by the middle of the next century the old-age pension will be a relative pittance, standing at something like 8 per cent of average earnings.

Bringing together the information just presented on the number of people who are dependent for their income on what taxpayers provide collectively through the state, we can consider what is going to happen to the relative value of the state pension. Its cost will continue to dominate the welfare budget, but it will increasingly give rise to an ever more inadequate income. Many people will lose much of their occupational pension because of unemployment, and for others private pension contracts will deliver only a meagre pension. Consider how the scope and value of SERPS has been curtailed and how difficult it is to reconcile the scenario of an unfolding pensions bliss with what will be happening in the real world. Indeed, a major pensions reform is necessary not in order to satisfy the Government's wish to cut government expenditure, but because the link between poverty and old age is far from broken for many individuals and is being re-linked for all too many others. Indeed, it is possible that we will see a growing proportion of pensioners with additional income from private schemes but, because of the limited size of these payments and the fall in the relative value of the flat-rate state pension to earnings, a greater number of them will have an income of only a little, if anything, above the state minimum income support level. Pension reform is therefore a matter of urgency.

A key assumption in mapping out such a reform is that no welfare structure can succeed unless full employment is regained. That phrase needs to be emphasized for, while an increasing number of politicians are thankfully beginning to register the need for full employment and to take on board the link between full employment and delivering a successful welfare strategy, nobody is considering a welfare scenario where full employment is not achieved.

At the last election Labour pledged to raise old-age pensions by £8 for married couples and £5 for the single pensioner. The cost of this move would have added an extra £2.5 billion to public expenditure each year (and a similar amount to the tax burden). The poorest pensioners would have gained nothing from such a move. The right hand of the state would have handed them a flat-rate pension increase and the left hand of the state would have taken an equal amount back from income support payments. Moreover, a universal increase in pensions for today's pensioners builds in the increase into the scheme so that the new level of benefit will be paid to all future pensioners, irrespective of their income. In the event, the electorate decided not to buy this approach. The 1992 election therefore probably marks the last occasion when a major political party put forward an additional, across-the-board increase in the flat-rate National Insurance pension.

The information given earlier on the age distribution of the poorest pensioners shows that, while there is a spread of such pensioners through each of the age groups, poorer pensioners are, generally speaking, likely to be the oldest. It was this group that was too old to gain membership of SERPS and which was doubly penalized by firms not offering occupational pensions. Additional pension increases need to be targeted to this group. Official figures show the failure of the Government's approach in its targeting strategy. Additional help is offered to the poorest pensioners by way of income support, but the official figures show that something in the region of a million pensioners do not claim the help to which they are entitled under this scheme. Another way forward must be found.

The SERPS scheme offers such an advance. Whilst it would be possible to credit into SERPS the oldest pensioners and to give them a generous entitlement, such an approach has its difficulties. One concern is that any additional help offered to the poorest pensioners may discourage other people of working age from providing adequately for their retirement. That difficulty needs to be faced squarely.

As part of the overall pension reform being advocated here, it is proposed that over a period of time it shall become compulsory for all employees to be members of an additional pension scheme whether it be final salary, a money-purchase scheme or a portable personal pension. Moreover, during this period of time it should become compulsory for employers to make a minimum contribution to this additional pension scheme. Part-time workers would be brought within the scope of the reform with contributions based on the number of hours worked, starting with the first hour. The incentive, therefore, to employ only part-time workers (much diminished with the National Insurance contribution changes advocated here) will be eliminated.

Seen as part of a comprehensive pension reform, crediting the oldest, frailest pensioners into SERPS is therefore likely to have only little, if any, backlash from the electors. It is a proposal, however, whose advantages go beyond successfully targeting help for those of lowest incomes. SERPS entitlement dies with the pensioner. As a result, this particular reform not only offers the advantages which come with targeting, but limits costs to a set number of years. This contrasts starkly to any increase in the basic rate of the old-age pension which, once enacted, not only helps today's pensioners but every succeeding generation of pensioners irrespective of their income from other sources.

One last point with respect to pension reforms. At the end of this chapter, when reforms for today's unemployed are considered, a proposal is set out to allow taxpayers to make contributions to the private pension schemes for those who are unemployed. Not only does this proposal mean a spreading of the cost of unemployment more fairly; it is equally important as a move which will help prevent many of today's unemployed from becoming poor in old age.

Single Mums and Dads

A second group, a large proportion of whose members are likely to remain on welfare for a long if not indefinite period, are single parent families. Within a space of twenty years the number of single parents has more than doubled: from 570,000 in 1971 to 1.3 million in 1991. Of all the European Community countries Britain, along with Denmark, has the highest proportion of single parents. The fastest growing group of single parents, as the graph (see page 92) shows, are those who have never married. Here numbers have risen since 1971 from 90,000 to 440,000. The next most significant group of single parents are divorced people whose numbers have grown from 120,000 to 430,000 over the same period.

It is the increase in the numbers of unmarried mothers which should cause the most concern. It is in this group that the greatest dependency on benefits is found. Nine out of ten single mothers claim income support and, as an entire group, they make up over 4 in 10 of all single parents drawing benefit. Generally speaking, they are of a younger age group than other single parents. As a group they are the least likely to be in receipt of maintenance payments, the least likely to remain in contact with the father of their child, to know his whereabouts, or even to know who he is.

Overall, the propensity of lone parents to be claiming income support has increased: in 1991 around two-thirds of lone parents were claiming income support compared with two-fifths claiming supplementary benfits ten years previously. This reflects, in part at least, the growing proportion of lone parents who are single or separated mothers. Over 90 per cent of this group presently claim benefits compared with two-fifths of divorced mothers and lone fathers and one-sixth of widowed mothers.

More generally, all groups of lone parents appear to be more likely to be claimants now than ten years previously. The number of lone parents claiming income support is likely to continue to grow both because of the increase in the total number of one-parent families and because of an increase in the proportion of this group who are single and separated mothers – those most likely to be claimants. Even if there is no other increase in the propensity of lone parents claiming benefit, the number of one-parent families in receipt of income support is likely to grow by a quarter of a million in the five years up to 1996 and by half a million over the whole of the decade up to 2001, giving a total of around 1.8 million on benefit.

Now to the figures relating to the most vulnerable of mothers – those under sixteen. Eight thousand girls under sixteen gave birth last year. Mothers under sixteen have no right to claim benefit under their own names. If the young mother's family is on benefit they continue to be classified as a dependent of that family. So does their child.

Of these worrying figures, the increase in the number of very young mothers is the trend which causes the most concern. Many people who quote figures on unmarried mothers assume that we have lost a golden age when almost every married couple lived happily ever after. The truth is that some did and some didn't. I take my great-grandparents as an example. Confusion has always reigned in my mind about

Lone parents in receipt of Supplementary Benefit/Income Support
GREAT BRITAIN; *(000's)**

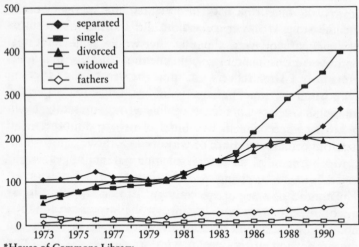

*House of Commons Library

who was married to whom, who were half-brothers and sisters, who then became step-cousins and so on. The reason for this? Death struck earlier then. Widowhood was much more common, as was remarriage. My grandmother and great-aunts talked of widowers with silk umbrellas. Widows would expect to remarry and to marry widowers, and the silk umbrella signified that the potential partner had some financial assets to bring to the marriage. So marriage then was different from now in the crucial respect that it would last on average for less than fifteen years. Death would bring it to a close and then emotional, as well as economic pressures, would necessitate a new partnership. Few of our great-grandparents ever expected that they would be called upon to honour their marriage vows over fifty or sixty years, as growing life expectancy dictates now. How many of our great-grandparents would have been able to live up to that ideal is anybody's guess.

But this tale is not given in order to encourage complacency, rather to suggest what any set of figures can hide as well as reveal. There is another important difference between what went on in the time of my great-grandparents and today. The position of the children of the marriage was very different. Death had taken one of their parents. That parent hadn't decided to walk off preferring to build another life without their family. Moreover, a 'new' father would as likely as not soon appear on the scene together with a tribe of additional brothers and sisters.

We simply do not know the consequences of the break-up of families on the scale we are now experiencing. It may have no lasting effect whatsoever, but I somehow doubt it. It is therefore prudent to think of ways by which we can sustain two-parent families, as well as single-parent families, during a period when a growing proportion of marriages end in divorce, and how we can encourage them to make as big a success of their lives as they can. At the same time we must consider how best to prevent single-parenthood and the collapse of the family.

Here a range of policies is necessary, but I don't believe they will be successful in reducing the number and percentage of young single mothers unless, and until, the economy returns to full employment. At fifty I am no older than some of the grandparents of the single teenage mothers I represent as an MP. I am aware of some of the barriers these young people feel in talking to someone as old as I am, especially on issues which concern their private life. But one point which is made repeatedly is that for some very young women, starting a family is the only option they have. Their sisters (some of whom are single parents) have been on not one, but two, three or more training courses and still have no job at the end of it all. And while more middle-class girls may think that having a child, claiming welfare and getting a council flat is the start of a life of Riley, few of the poorer mothers ever express such an illusion. They know only too well what life is like on welfare from watching their mothers (only a minority at the time of conception are still living with both their parents) battling with authority. Neither do they have any illusions about the kind of flat they will be offered by the local council. They will fight like mad to get as good a home as possible – they will see me, lobby councillors and plead over the counter in the housing office – but they nevertheless know that in the end the chances are that they will be put on a sink estate. They do, however, express surprise at what hard work it is looking after themselves and their baby. That their own mothers play a crucial part in their survival is not in doubt. Those who lack this support are the most vulnerable of all single mothers.

What can be done? To stress the need for jobs does not mean that there are no other policies worth pursuing. It means that other reforms will be less effective until every young woman is given the option to work rather than that of immediately starting a family.

The first step is to spread the success of a project which operates from Bristol. At Barton Hill very young mothers go back into schools to tell pupils what it's like being sixteen or seventeen, housed on a sink estate, the endless drudgery of trying to make ends meet, the efforts involved in keeping the baby healthy and clean, and the likelihood of depression as these pressures build up. Not only may the boyfriend have disappeared, but ex-friends (contact is soon lost with most school friends) will be out at nightclubs and generally enjoying themselves, while the single mother is at home trying to pacify her crying, demanding child. The Barton Hill project needs to be multiplied and put into operation all over the country.

Part of the school curriculum should centre on the workings of the new Child Support Agency. The present Government allowed the near collapse of the issuing of maintenance payments to mothers on welfare. Now there is much rejoicing in heaven as the Government has repented its sins and thrown its weight behind a new strategy to enforce maintenance payments for these mothers.

The new Child Support Agency which came into operation in April 1993 is responsible for not only laying down a set level of maintenance, but has powers to secure payments from the father of the child. The fact that the Government is taking seriously, and intends to put an end to, the non-payment of maintenance at least for those mothers on welfare, will begin to settle into the national consciousness. Such a move by itself is not going to prevent young people behaving irresponsibly, but, as part of an overall strategy, it has a part to play.

The real weakness of the child support agency is that, as presently constituted, it will do very little to ensure that maintenance payments are paid for those mothers who are *not* on welfare. One of my constituents describes the obstacles she faces in trying to leave welfare, build up a part-time job and be independent, when the father of her children refuses to pay maintenance. Up until April 1992 Margaret, responsible for two young children, was on income support and worked in a local bank for twenty hours a week. The bank paid her £85 a week, she gained around £43 in income support and as a result her two children were eligible for free school meals. Margaret takes up the story.

I have always been anxious to move off income support and therefore jumped at the opportunity presented to me when the rules changed in April 1992. I then became eligible for what is called family credit. Before changing over to family credit I asked the local DSS, as well as the housing benefit section of the local council, what level of poll tax I would be expected to pay once I ceased drawing income support. You will realize that while I was on income support the whole of my poll tax was in fact paid. Both the income support office and housing benefit section told me that I would pay slightly more, but certainly not the full amount.

While I was on income support I contributed £7 a month as a poll tax contribution. As soon as I claimed family credit this sum jumped to £44 a month. There was no way I could meet this sort of bill and I told the local council so. They advised me to continue paying

£7 a month. They added that things would sort themselves out. They have, but not in the way I thought. The local authority has issued a summons for non-payment even though I've been paying the £7 regularly.

The next hole I was landed in was the direct result of working an extra hour a day for five weeks during last summer. These weeks coincided with the period running up to a new claim for family credit. My new family credit book had the weekly amount reduced from £48 to £44.60 a week on the assumption that I would continue to earn £105 instead of the regular £85 I have always earned since returning to work at the bank. One small bonus of reduced family credit was that my poll tax demand was reduced from £44 a month to £36, but with family credit, unlike income support, I am not eligible for free school meals for my children.

My husband refuses to pay any maintenance although I must say his parents, and mine, do what they can for our children. I have given up taking my husband to court. I did get a maintenance order against him which he refused to pay. When I went to talk to my solicitor about this I was told 'Well, that's that.' I was equally surprised when I asked at the local court what I should do. They told me that most maintenance orders are not paid. I don't know whether this is true but it appears that only I thought my husband would be duty bound to meet the order laid down by the court. No one else did.

What has happened to Margaret illustrates the need for two further reforms. First of all, the new Child Support Agency needs to extend its scope to single mothers who are in work. The agency needs to be recast so that if mothers assign their maintenance orders to the agency, the mother will receive regularly the maintenance payments from the agency whether or not the agency is successful in gaining the sums from the father. At the moment the income of a mother on benefit is not affected if the father refuses to pay. She and her family continue to draw their full social security payments. Her income drops once she is back at work and the father refuses to pay maintenance. A new, major disincentive to return to work has been created.

Family credit also needs to be recast. It has been a much bigger success than many on the Left claimed it could be, but it is still highly inflexible. People like Margaret, who work for a few extra hours when the opportunity arises, must be able to do so without being penalized. The weeks during which she worked an extra five hours were wrongly used to calculate the amount of the next six months' family credit. If the department cannot move on from awarding benefit for six months only, it does need to take into account earnings over the whole of the previous six months, and not to rely arbitrarily on a few weeks preceding a new claim.

The Long-Term Dole Queue

Now to the third group forced onto long-term welfare dependency. Long-term unemployment is defined as being without work for over a year. There are over a million people who fall into this category, standing as they have been in dole queues for twelve months or more. If the slump were miraculously halted the number of unemployed, and with it the proportion of people in long-term unemployment, is likely to continue to rise for some time.

Even with the severity of today's slump, unemployment does not fall like God's gentle rain evenly over the whole country. It strikes from underneath and it hits hardest those who are already poor and on low incomes. So, while it is true this time round, as compared with the recessions of the early and mid-1980s, that people in the South are being attacked by unemployment on a scale beyond anything within living memory, unemployment generally remains worse in the northern parts of the country.

In both the North and the South unemployment affects

certain groups with equal devastation. But while unemployment has been visited on people who have held management positions for the whole of their working lives, and although it remains unbelievably difficult for them to gain a new post, their chances of finding work are still greater than those for people without skills. Yet it is still as true as ever that an unemployment rate of a single person is a total tragedy for that person without a job.

For some unskilled people the chances of finding work are slim both in the North and the South. Moreover, it is likely that other people in the same family will be without work, and also have only a slim chance of ever working again under the existing regime. Indeed, entire families face this prospect. For them, the impossibility of ever finding work has a profound effect on how they lead their lives.

There are two options available to those denied work year after year. One is to send oneself mad, looking, searching, pleading and scrambling after every rumour that a job may be lurking around the next corner, in the next newspaper advertisement, or on the next card in the job centre. And people, if not driven clinically mad, are beset with the deepest of depressions. Doctors prescribe anti-depressants knowing that what their patients need is work not drugs. Some families disintegrate as they are forced to witness a loved one driven demented by the endless but fruitless task of searching for employment.

The alternative approach is to accept that one will never work again. The simplest thing to do is to write out of one's life the whole idea of work itself. Life is then organized on the basis that no one in the household will ever have a paid job. What one can or cannot do will be determined largely by the rate of benefit. It will also be determined by what extra little help one's parents and even grandparents can give. And not surprisingly, the temptation to make something on the side becomes ever more attractive as debts mount. Life becomes about keeping debts under some sort of control, trying to have the smallest treats without sending the budget totally out of control, preventing one's marriage from totally disintegrating and trying to find the money to pay for the escalating bills which are now an integral part of our free education system: school uniforms, school trips, the cost of materials for courses. The one thing which must be forbidden is to start thinking about, let alone longing for, a job. All around one can see the devastation of people's lives once they have succumbed to that indulgence.

Policies are required at three different levels if any hope is to be held out to those who have been in the dole queues longest. First, there is the need to abate the present slump. Second is the task of negotiating the way back to full employment. If the first objective cannot be achieved immediately, this is even more true of the second objective. Both these areas are examined in more detail in the final chapter. The third policy, which I discuss here, is one which would deal with the immediate task of changing the order in which employers fill whatever vacancies are available.

As with the figures on single parents, the data on the long-term unemployed can hide information as well as reveal it. Not only have there been twenty-seven changes to the way the numbers of unemployed are counted – thereby nearly always reducing the official numbers recorded of the unemployed – but the way the length of time that people have been out of work is measured has been overhauled as well. Some of the schemes for the long-term unemployed result in individuals graduating from training courses without a job, and then being reclassified as short-term unemployed. Also, the Government used to collect and publish data on the number of unemployed drawing supplementary benefits (renamed income support in 1988) for up to ten years. Figures are now released only for unemployed claimants who have been on benefit for over five years. Even so, the total of 110,000 is staggering. The longer a person has been unemployed, the less the chance they have of gaining a job. It is as though Adam Smith's hidden hand keeps pushing the long-term unemployed further back in the queue.

What measures would help them gain a place at the front? Four reforms could be introduced with minimum cost to taxpayers. Indeed some would result in a net saving to the Treasury. The first small reform concerns the signing-off procedure. When a person gains a job they naturally surrender their right to the dole or income support. That is fine if the job is permanent and does in fact live up to expectations. Re-registering for benefit can take weeks, and no money is paid out until the re-registering has been successful. This rule therefore deters unemployed people from taking a risk by accepting perhaps a temporary job and seeing whether, once inside the firm, they can negotiate a more permanent post. The Government should consider allowing people to suspend their right to benefit for a period of time, then employment could be accepted with the sure knowledge that, should the job fold, benefit would be restored (after the production of the pay-slips earned in the meantime).

A second minor, but significant, reform concerns changes to the National Insurance scheme. Workers earning below £56 a week pay no National Insurance contributions. Nor do their employers. The National Insurance contributory scheme is rigging the labour market in favour of part-time jobs. The Government should introduce as a matter of urgency a reform of the National Insurance system which would collect employers' contributions from the first pound of earnings. As the proposal is not meant to be revenue raising the employer contribution on other workers would be therefore marginally reduced. A level playing field would be created and it would be up to employers and employees to work out for themselves the package of hours that would be offered by the employer and the number of hours that would be acceptable to the employee. Offering full, semi-full, or part-time work would carry neither penalties, nor advantages to the employer.

Now to proposals that attempt to beat employer resistance to taking on those who have been standing in the dole queue for longest. Here the Government has begun to act but its very limited actions need to be pushed much more imaginatively. In the 1993 Budget the Government announced that it had established a pilot study in four areas to test the effectiveness of a wage subsidy for long-term unemployed. Employers taking on claimants who have been without work for over two years are entitled to a £60-a-week subsidy.

To this rather timid reform needs to be added a whole series of other reform experiments aimed at countering the imagined disadvantage for employers taking on workers who have become long-term unemployed. The proposal this time round for a wage subsidy has come from Professor Dennis Snowner. On his calculations the Government could offer a £150 subsidy and still not add to the taxpayer's bill. Experiments with such a level of subsidy should be initiated immediately.

The idea of a direct wage subsidy should then be matched by other pilot studies which empower the unemployed when seeking work. Here the Government should experiment with the idea that those unemployed for over, say, five years should be entitled to keep their benefit for an entire year once they have gained a job paying at least £60 a week. This proposal would put power into the hands of the unemployed enabling them to tackle employers directly and bargain for a marginal job. The advantages of the proposal are fairly obvious. Once inside a firm the ex-unemployed will hear of other job opportunities. The proposal will offer a chance of a much higher income coming into the household. It would allow partners to work without the benefit rules penalizing them. It would also save the taxpayers money in that all the income from earnings and benefit would be liable to tax. Likewise, it would discourage the black market.

A similar proposal would be to issue wage vouchers to the unemployed for a given amount which they could take with them when bargaining for a job opportunity. The voucher, which might vary from anything between £60 and £150 a week, would be cashed by employers once they had taken any long-term unemployed person onto their books. This proposal has the advantage of empowering the unemployed while allowing them to seek jobs at market rates above their benefit entitlement, and of encouraging employers to employ those who have been on the dole longest.

A wage subsidy scheme could also be set up, provided an employer, when taking on a long-term unemployed person, was prepared to spend the whole of the wage subsidy on giving the person training. Here the proposal would test the view that long-term unemployed people lose their work skills, have difficulty in meeting a work routine, and consequently are of less value to the employer. The training subsidy would aim to raise their productivity to equal that of other members in the firm.

Throughout this book the importance of full employment and the achievement of full employment is stressed repeatedly, and this is the theme of the last chapter. An increasing number in work not only has an immediate impact on the income of a larger number of individuals at the bottom of the income pile, not only has an immediate impact on both the size and the distribution of the welfare budget, but also opens up the possibility of rebuilding lost contributions to future (pension) income. The impact on the income of the unemployed and the welfare budget are considered later.

Every government statement makes plain that the overall aim of economic policy has been to control inflation by increasing the level of unemployment – not directly, of course, but every rise in interest rates has meant that while some firms have shed labour, others have simply closed. Among the proposals in the final chapter for regaining full employment is the idea of work-sharing. As well as sharing work the cost of unemployment could be shared by imposing an unemployment tax on those in work so that more generous benefits could be paid to those out of work.

While the recruiting sergeants have been busily conscripting people into an unemployment army in order to fight inflation, the rations of this army have been cut on numerous occasions. The unemployed have suffered benefit reductions: since 1979 there have been almost forty changes in unemployment benefit, reducing the income of Britain's jobless.

Levying a specific unemployment tax will have an impact on public debate in two important ways. It will bring home to the wider electorate that there is an immediate cost to unemployment, that this is currently being disproportionately borne by the unemployed and should henceforth be shared more equally. This means that the main beneficiaries of low inflation – the employed – should pay a higher price for that privilege. The levy of a special unemployment tax will also introduce a sense of urgency currently lacking in the political debate to finding ways of returning to full employment, which would, thereby, reduce taxes.

The proposal is for unemployment benefit to be raised to the same level of invalidity benefit – an increase for a single person and a married couple of £11.05 and £17 respectively a week. The cost of this move would be in the region of £400 million. The unemployment tax should also cover the cost of maintaining the pension contributions of the unemployed both to the state scheme and to occupational and personal schemes. The cost of this reform is estimated to be in the region of £500 million pounds. Reform is also urgent for those who are already pensioners and who are not entitled to SERPS or occupational pensions.

Conclusion

Britain's welfare budget has expanded and continues to expand, but should be reduced. The aim of any reduction should not be, as with the present Tory Government, to make poorer people worse off so that taxes for better-off people can be cut. The radical aim must be to provide a whole range of exits from welfare dependency for those three groups which have been described as being on 'the other side' of the United Kingdom. That is clearly impossible for those who are already retired and therefore have no opportunity whatsoever to build a capital base as a by-product of work. What is clear, however, is that no party is going to stand on a programme of universally increasing the state old-age pension to a level adequate enough to free the least privileged pensioners from their poverty. It is gesture politics of the worst order to pretend otherwise. More selective approaches are therefore necessary. In respect to single-mothers, policies are advocated here which attempt both to dry up the supply routes to single parenthood, particularly amongst very young single women, and at the same time to build a whole range of exits for those single mothers on benefit. But here, as with the reforms for the unemployed, the approach is a mere palliative unless a policy of full employment is simultaneously embarked upon. Indeed, full employment as an objective is crucial. No discussion is currently taking place about what welfare payments are possible if Britain continues to insist that millions of individuals should remain out of work for decade upon decade. There are, of course, ways of sharing more equitably the cost of unemployment and these have been suggested. But the objective of full employment is at the heart of the new radicalism advocated in this book and it is that topic to which the final chapter is devoted. But first we need to consider the ownership of pension funds and how reforms here have a part to play in re-establishing full employment.

CHAPTER FIVE

Labour: The Party of Work, Wealth and Opportunity

The last two chapters have been concerned with the worst casualties of post-war welfare policies. Currently eighty billion pounds is spent annually on welfare payments, but the number of casualties continues to rise. There is a need for an urgent rethink about our system of welfare which has for nearly two centuries picked up the industrial system's casualties. A successful welfare strategy should focus on the production and distribution of wealth with the aim to set up policies which link a growing number of people into that success which comes from working and owning wealth. Success in the traditional welfare field should therefore be marked by reductions in the welfare budget as increasing numbers of people have their incomes determined by work or wealth.

Shared by the Safety Net

Since the 1834 Poor Law Reform Act welfare has been explicitly about making good the failure of industrialism to provided a minimum income for the entire population. The campaign around the turn of the century for unemployment insurance and old-age pensions was no new departure: it was essentially a continuation of the approach of applying bandages to bind up the wounds inflicted by capitalism which had failed to deliver the goods. The pre-World War One Lloyd George reforms, and their continuation during the inter-war years by Neville Chamberlain, are all part of the same story. The Beveridge Report was not an innovation, but a supremely successful operation of locking the political debate into this approach. All post-war proposals for reform have been about rectifying the perceived deficiencies of the Beveridge scheme. Our age demands a radically new approach.

Over the past two centuries the approach of policy makers and politicians has been first to define who is poor and second to devise welfare benefits which would lessen their deprivation. A totally new starting point would be to ask how we can make sure that the pressures which have held people in inescapable poverty are overcome. All but the most stubborn of politicians know that the best way of freeing people from the indenture of dependency is by locking them into the nation's wealth. The same mechanism of a mounting GDP was able to remove the fear of starvation from our shores two hundred years ago and has enabled the living standards of everyone, and particularly the lucky majority, to soar.

When we open up a long overdue debate about the basis of welfare, the first question asked must be why is this miraculous mechanism still failing many people? Secondly, we must ask why the bureaucracies which we have built to guard against such failure are performing so poorly.

For the Left, the defence of welfare 'above all else' is a worthy and convenient slogan. It seems almost common-sensical to celebrate the flourishing garden which Mr Beveridge sowed. But if we are serious about helping people to achieve self-betterment can we really defend a system that offers so many people so little chance of change?

We must realize that the growth of the welfare budget is not a criterion by which to measure success. An expanding welfare system is a failing welfare system – not because of any deep faith in the philosophies of the minimalist state, but because it means people are being dragged down and snared in the safety net. Welfare can no longer be expected to clean up the deprivation national wealth has failed to ensure against. New ideas in every area of welfare provision are needed; radical reform is vital.

The Centrality of Pensions

Here I take pension provision to illustrate an approach which I believe should be followed across the welfare field. Pension provision is used as an example because it commands a larger part of GDP than any other benefit, has developed a very substantial private sector provision and because the assets of private sector schemes act as a bridge between welfare and industrial policy. Welfare in this case is naturally recast as a key part of industrial strategy. Any discussion of welfare should be not only about the welfare of pensioners, and potential pensioners, important as that is, but should form part of the national debate about Britain's industrial recovery.

The first industrial pension scheme commenced in the Civil Service in the 1850s. By the end of the century a number of employers were providing past employees with what were the first occupational pensions. These sums were modest, and, rather than attempting to extend their coverage or raise the value of these payments, reformers' efforts centred on persuading the State to introduce a system of old-age pensions. The successful implementation of the first old-age pensions in 1908 was followed by a number of reforms carried out during the inter-war years. These were milestones on the way to the measures which culminated in the Beveridge scheme, and then in the ill-fated Crossman reforms and finally the State Earnings Related Pension Scheme – or SERPS.

While most public attention during this century's long debate was focused on what the politicians were either promising or trying to deliver, companies were quietly getting on with the job of spreading their wealth both to workers in the form of pensions, and to owners in the form of dividends. The end product has been one of the most significant but least appreciated successes of industrialism: almost sixteen million people are now in schemes with pension funds and allied portfolios which account for a staggering fifty per cent of all quoted shares in this country. It has consequently been estimated that the top fifty pension fund managers have effective control of UK industry through the capital base which our occupational pensions funds own.

These funds are held in two types of private pension provision. The first is the final salary scheme. This is, as the name suggests, a pension which is wage related, normally aiming to provide a pension at half or two-thirds of the contributor's final wage or salary. This scheme is tripartite, with employers, employees and taxpayers (by way of handsome tax reliefs) making contributions. The other main type of pension is the money purchase scheme whereby a sum is built up by the employee with the help of the taxpayer and sometimes the employer. This can be run as an occupational pension or as a personal portable pension. The size of a final pension is not guaranteed but is totally dependent on the amount saved and the value of the annuities which can be bought with the savings at the point of retirement.

Earnings from these two types of pension schemes have successfully provided a growing income for pensioners and will be expected to do the same for an increasing proportion of retired scheme members. Furthermore, that proportion is set to rise inexorably as a greater number of workers who are already in schemes become eligible for the benefits of occupational pensions. With such a successful record, why should the issue of reform even be raised?

That question can be answered succinctly. The £254 billion of pension fund assets might as well be nationalized as far as pension holders are concerned. They are told that this wealth is largely theirs, but only some of the advantages of wealth ownership actually accrues to them. In respect of pension wealth, the population is treated in law exactly the same way as were women, children and lunatics until very recently – they were not seen as responsible enough to be trusted with ownership. Now only lunatics and pension fund members are viewed as unable to look after their own affairs.

New Demands and New Opportunities

The cry for reform is raised on narrow welfare grounds too. The coverage of occupational schemes is incomplete and new disenfranchized groups are already appearing on the horizon. As we saw in the last chapter, the oldest and frailest pensioners gained nothing from SERPS from past employers. Their crime is one of age: they were too old to be included in either type of scheme. As this group dies its shoes will be filled by another group of disenfranchized pensioners: the unemployed. 'Retired' ten or even twenty years early, this group witnesses much of its entitlement to an occupational pension whittled away. Unemployment, in other words, not only excludes this group from an adequate income now but from a share in future pension wealth and the welfare that that brings.

There also appears to be a glass ceiling operating against the spread of occupational schemes. I would guess (there are no studies) that newly established employers are not offering an occupational pension. There is also an employment trend in many successful companies whereby new jobs are awarded part-time status and an employment contract which excludes the holder from membership of the company's pension scheme. Firms have also been hiving off some of their operations to newly formed independent companies. Many of these new ventures have looked critically at the provision of company welfare and at the daunting risk of providing final salary schemes.

Reforms must be implemented to prevent pension fund assets from being engulfed in a three-fold crisis, which has been stealing up on these schemes over the past few years. Each one of these forces or crises makes for change. The 1980s, generally speaking, was a decade of economic growth, a fact reflected in dividend payments. The bonfire of financial restrictions, combined with the relaxation of monetary control, resulted in major capital gains accruing to pension portfolios. Moreover these capital gains and dividend payments were in part responsible for the build up in most funds of substantial surpluses. The harsh treatment of those who left a scheme before they retired was another contributing factor. (This coming decade is unlikely to see a similar combination leading to the boosting of pension funds.) In 1986 the Government began taxing any surplus which was 105 per cent above the pension fund's liabilities. The taking of pension holidays, as they are euphemistically called, has become a widespread practice. The surpluses are still in the process of being cut.

The difficulties in the performance of the real economy and falling surpluses are coinciding at a time when the demands of pension funds are likely to increase. The Barber Judgement on non-discrimination heightens the looming crisis which, together with similar cases which are awaited from the European Court, will have a major impact on pension fund finances.

The consequence is already plain to see: the move from final salary to money purchase schemes is underway, and is likely to become widespread. The conventional wisdom is that this is a retrograde move. That view should be challenged – in particular by those who want to shift the debate from welfare to wealth. It is far easier to transfer ownership to individual members of money purchase schemes.

Recognizing Ownership

Let me put the argument another way. The spread of final salary schemes appears to have reached a peak. Some final salary schemes will run into trouble during this decade. Employers will be reluctant, and some unable, to pick up the deficits, as they are required to do by law. A rethink is urgent and should centre on the ownership of funds.

The majority of firms in which people work are owned by somebody else's pension fund – but not that of the pensioners themselves, or of future pensioners. As with nationalized

110

industries, which no one in their right mind thought were owned by us, so too with our 'own' pension funds.

A truly radical pension reform should follow three political objectives:

— a new form of collectivism which owes nothing to state control or imposition, and everything to the actions of individuals who freely opt for it;
— a means by which consumer power begins to give British industry the financial stability which has been so beneficial to our Japanese and German competitors;
— a truly revolutionary redistribution in the ownership of capital which owes nothing to increasing taxes but which has the potential to make the sale of council houses appear as a feeble dress-rehearsal.

Pension reform should aim at nothing less than the abolition of pension serfdom whereby people's capital assets are not owned by them. Reform should seek to give people control over their own pension capital, whether or not they remain with one employer all their lives.

This goal must be accomplished in stages to ensure that today's success (whereby a growing number of people have a generous occupational pension once they retire) becomes an even greater success for even more people who have not only an adequate retirement income but also gain an ownership of the pension fund which is currently denied to members.

Stage one of the reform is to cease peddling the propaganda of the pensions industry, much of which centres on selling the final salary approach. Yet, very few pensioners have so far retired with a pension at that level. Most people have not been in the schemes long enough to qualify, or have had to move out of a pension fund each time they have changed their job. Stage two is to accept that in the immediate future any spread of private pension schemes will come from a growing popularity of money purchase schemes. These schemes have two drawbacks: the first is that the resulting pension depends on the size of the sum which has been built up by regular contributions – the larger the sum the larger will be the pension income. The second stage concerns the timing of when these funds are transferred from investments into annuities to guarantee regular pension payments. Timing can be crucial to the size of the pension. If, for example, an annuity was bought on Friday 23 October 1987 the resulting pension would have been 30 per cent less than if it had been bought a week earlier. The reason? Between these two dates there was a major collapse in stock market prices.

Two further moves can improve substantially the size of a pension which results from money purchase schemes. The first is to compel employers to match the contributions made by their employees. The standard New Right response that this will mean a tax on jobs and that employment will be driven abroad will immediately ring out. While this must be a concern, the cry of job losses should not automatically result in voters becoming mesmerized like rabbits in the line of oncoming headlights. There are already considerable numbers of employers who already make such contributions. Moreover, there is the example of Australia where legislation has made such employer contributions compulsory. And that has been achieved without the dire consequences claimed by Britain's industrial Jeremiahs.

The second initiative is to ensure that the value of an individual's pension fund is not determined by the fund's realization at an unfavourable moment when, perhaps, asset prices are falling. If capital-generating assets for each individual are transferred into income-generating assets over a longish period of time, the risk of sharp falls in capital assets will be mitigated.

Stage three is to reform the final salary scheme membership. Again, this will need to be taken in steps. Ownership of pension funds is the central question being considered by the Goode committee which will report in the autumn of 1993.

The report will be followed by debates, consultations, and then legislation. What is crucial is to seize the opportunity to begin constructing a new ownership for final salary schemes. A clear choice will have to be made. If final salary schemes are to be maintained on the principle that employers are responsible for making good the deficit which may arise in the fund, then employers will understandably claim the right to any surplus and, understandably enough, to a control of the size of benefits paid out of the scheme. A legal framework which enables employers to draw upon surpluses and to close schemes rather than to make up benefits is clearly unsatisfactory as we attempt to provide more and more people with the benefits of holding substantial assets.

I, therefore, favour a fundamental reform of pension law, the success of which would in part depend on the degree to which employers would be willing to participate in shaping the new reforms. The aim should be for tripartite ownership, with employer, worker and pensioner interests all represented. The surrender by employers of their control over the funds has to be matched by an acceptance that they are not going to add additional fund contributions in order to achieve pensions of two-thirds final salary when such contributions may become necessary. For the reasons to which I have already alluded, I believe some employers will be unwilling to meet this commitment under the existing legal framework. Other employers – all too thoughtlessly dismissed as paternalistic – will attempt to fund schemes so that the two-thirds final salary will be the object for pension payments. But once a new ownership of funds is agreed it will be open to the three groups owning the funds, and not merely the employer, to agree contribution levels which will fund final salary pension levels. If reform is likely to go in this direction it is possible to see the growing together of final salary and money purchase schemes.

Stage four follows from this new ownership structure. As soon as workers and pensioners have direct representation on the final salary scheme trusts, the question arises of how these representatives should be appointed. I favour direct election. There will be arguments made against such a line, following those which have challenged any extension of the franchise. These arguments should be vigorously opposed.

Once these different reforms have been accomplished an individual will have a range of choices about how and when to manage his substantial pension assets. Such choice will be applicable to both final salary and money purchase schemes, as well as to portable pensions. Many, if not most, individuals will want to keep their assets as part of the company scheme. Alternatively, they may wish to arrange this investment through private sector investment firms.

It is at this point that the possibility of a new kind of Left politics arises. These reforms give the Left the golden opportunity to win approval for a collective response which has nothing to do with the state and everything to do with the options freely made by members of pension schemes. Trade unions could, if they wanted, compete to hold these pension funds by forming themselves into friendly societies. The next fifty years could become the age of voluntary friendly societies, in contrast to the centring on state activity which has dominated much of this century so far. Seizing the initiative offered by this long overdue reform of pension fund law not merely changes the welfare scene but offers a new balance between individualism, the state's role, and non-state collective action.

Trade unions would once again have a real job to do. Going back to their friendly society roots, they would need to buy in the necessary financial expertise for managing pension fund assets. Welfare reform and an industrial strategy for Britain would become interchangeable, especially since pension funds already own half of all British quoted companies.

The Concealed Power of Pensions

With so much of the equity market owned by pension funds, the big fund managers play a role in the modern industrial state similar to that of their baronial counterparts in medieval society. The actions of today's 'medieval barons' are, however, determined by their performance in the pension league table: the all-important question is whether their performance puts them in the top half of the table or not.

Here lies the root of the short-termism which has so bedeviled British industry, a short-termism which is largely inflicted by firms on one another. Every company demands that its pension fund outperforms the average, when only half can do so at any one time. Companies cannot, or rather should not, complain when fund managers seek to capitalize on takeover bids by selling their stake to the predator.

The effective ownership of companies by the pensioners and workforce would bring about the most profound change imaginable in the attitudes of each to Britain's industrial performance, the need for long-term industrial prosperity, and the breaking down once and for all of the 'them and us' mentality in British society. Workers or pensioners are going to have a different perspective about how well pension assets are performing. The league tables of those who boast of making most out of capital gains and immediate dividend advances will be downgraded. The emphasis will be much more like that in Japan where a long-term view – perhaps looking ahead to twenty years or more – of the likely growth in the value of pension assets and the income derived from them is taken. If ever there was an illustration of how self-interest can be organized to promote the common good this is it.

Pension Reform and Industrial Strategy

What would be the consequences of this reform which sees welfare expenditure primarily in terms of locking people into the country's wealth base? The impact on the welfare budget would be as dramatic as the impact on our attitudes to British industry. The country would be engaged in a joint endeavour of spreading the occupational pension success to a growing proportion of the workforce. If that took effect there would be a major knock-on effect on the national insurance pension scheme – or what is generally referred to as the old-age pension. This takes the arguments presented in the previous chapter on to a further stage.

As far as I am concerned there would never be any question of taking the right to the old-age pension away from anyone. But in the scenario I describe it would be legitimate to question whether each year the entire pensioner population should have their old age pension upgraded in line with prices. Consider two pieces of information.

First, social security expenditure takes over 30 per cent of government expenditure, and pensions alone take over two-fifths of that bill. The 1993 uprating of all benefits cost two and a half billion pounds. Pension increases cornered one billion of that sum. The increases were in effect universal, and made very little difference to the living standards of either the richest or the poorest pensioners.

Second, the richest 10 per cent of pensioners have an income of over six times more than the poorest. Even without the changes I have outlined there is a question to be answered here. Should future uprating increases go to rich and poor pensioners alike? Or should the whole of the increase for each year's uprating go to the poorest pensioners alone?

Conclusion

Labour has established a Social Justice Commission in order radically to review its welfare policies. It is crucial that the commission interprets its terms of reference in the broadest possible way. Welfare should be taken out of the ghetto and placed firmly as part of the debate on Britain's economic and industrial future. Instead of seeing welfare as a way of shoring up the failures of industrial systems, people should be locked into the success that comes from work and ownership of wealth. Once this is achieved the debate about reforming welfare assumes totally different proportions. This chapter has discussed how that approach can be initiated in respect of pensions. The debate needs to be conducted simultaneously in all other major areas of welfare expenditure. My aim has been to illustrate the potential for redistribution in our society, and to show how the main forms of redistribution to be enacted by a future Labour government do not involve the imposition of taxes. The debate should be about redistributing resources within the private sector and should not be limited to welfare alone.

This approach, which sees welfare as a crucial element in Britain's industrial policy, must itself be part of a much wider rethink of party policy. Fundamental to the success of the kind of welfare review advocated here is a determined attempt to achieve full employment. As in the welfare field, the language used by participants in this debate now stifles radical thinking. The intellectual challenge of how to achieve full employment is greater today than it was in the 1930s. It will require a degree of intellectual and political commitment which has yet to be demonstrated on the contemporary British scene. The beginnings of a march back to full employment are discussed in the following chapter.

CHAPTER SIX

The Forgotten Goal of Full Employment

The elimination of full employment as the major objective of economic policy has been the most silent and deadliest of Mrs Thatcher's revolutions. It has done more than any other single government act to pauperize many of our fellow citizens and rob them of a sense of dignity and worth. And yet there is no debate let alone challenge on this issue. Why has there been such an intellectual and political collapse on this front? Restoring full employment is no easy objective. Indeed, such has been the opposing campaign that many now believe this to be impossible. What are the immediate moves that the government could take in order to establish a level of unemployment below 500,000 as a major objective of home policy?

The Post-War Achievement

The immediate post-war years tell of a success. For the first time ever western Europe experienced a period of full employment. There had, of course, been times at the height of the boom when practically everyone who wanted to work could do so, but there had never been such a sustained period when those wishing to work had been able to.

This golden period, for that is how it appears now, lasted well into the 1960s. Events then changed swiftly. Unemployment, which had fluctuated at around 300,000 in the early post-war period, had doubled by January 1967. The upward movement had begun, rising to over 1 million early on in the Heath Government, to 1.5 million by mid-1976, and to

3 million in 1982. That too is today's figure. While almost all forecasters believe that there may be some economic recovery during 1993, none predicts that growth will be strong enough to prevent unemployment from mounting still further. Unemployment is set to rise well above the 3 million mark.

This tale of woe is merely the presentation of the official statistics. Since 1979 there have been twenty-seven changes in the way these data are computed, and almost all have resulted in a downward push in the numbers who appear in the official count. To give an accurate figure would mean adding something like a million to today's total.

Behind the Massed Aggregates

Leave aside these totals for a moment, as the numbers are hard to visualize. They also numb the mind to the human cost of unemployment. Of course, in the three or four million unemployed there will be a variety of individuals reacting in different ways to being made redundant. There will also be many young people – for unemployment is now heavily concentrated among this age group – who may never have had a job since leaving school. Some present a brave face. Indeed, that may be a true reflection of how those individuals feel. It is not my experience, though, in representing a seat which is cursed with a huge tally of people who have been conscripted into Britain's unemployment army.

Very few at the point of unemployment have trusted themselves (or perhaps me) to say what their true feelings were about being unemployed. Once they have managed to scramble out of the quagmire the impressions are easier to give: for example, despising oneself for not being able to find a job, the simple despair of writing to literally hundreds of employers, never to receive a reply. That constant struggle to get up in the morning, and finally not managing it, is another common experience; to shave or not to shave becomes one of the big questions of the day.

One of my constituents, Dave Christian, became un-employed in 1979 and recently described how that period felt. Not having any qualifications, he accepted the line that training and further qualifications would lead to a job. Ten years later this finally proved to be true when he was appointed to a post in the Probation Service. Dave takes up the story.

The gradual realization of the difficulties of finding a job on Merseyside was a frightening experience. The items we had gathered together for building a home of our own were slowly sold off. My name was on the waiting-list for work at every employer known to me in the area. I spent endless hours knocking on doors, writing letters and making telephone calls, but to no avail. I applied for any job that I heard of regardless of its locality.

Being without any money, except to meet the most basic needs, means you stop being a participant in society and become merely an observer of others. This, more than the mind-numbing boredom, the lack of money or the daily struggle to find a reason to get out of bed, shave or maintain an appearance, was what I found hardest to bear.

Long-term unemployment took its toll in a number of ways. First of all and most obvious to people is attempting to maintain a decent life on a very low income. Once all the saleable items that you own are gone you are at the mercy of the state benefit system. It would be wrong to say that you cannot survive on these benefits, but it would be right to say that this is just about as much as you can do. It is possible to eat basically and occasionally to buy cheap clothing and to pay essential bills. However, to anyone outside a monastery or prison, it is difficult to do no more with your life than this and still remain sane. It is difficult to maintain friendships when your finances allow no more active a life than watching TV. Very soon you are spending most of your time sitting in the living room or lying in bed. The tension of constantly living on top of each other, and the lack of diversion is one that I witnessed pull many relationships apart. I could sometimes go days without leaving the house, only going out eventually to visit the job centre or sign on. There is, of course, a limit to how long at any one stretch you can live like this. Sooner or later the time will come when you have to say 'bugger the consequences we are going for a night out' or 'lets buy in some really tasty food' or you will overspend on the kids' Christmas presents.

After Christmas 1979 it was not until 1989 that my wife or I bought each other a present, for Christmas, or birthdays, or anniversaries or any other time. The trouble is that the very next day you regret it. The money that you spent has to be found from somewhere and so you get behind with rent, in arrears with gas, electric, or the rates and eventually you fall victim to the high-interest loan merchants. So starts a cycle of debt that is impossible to get out of. The longer the period of unemployment the more frequent the lapses from basic life and therefore the deeper in debt you are. One of the harshest aspects of this is that basic living costs are higher when unemployed. The house requires heating all through the day, far more electricity is used through watching TV and drinking tea all day, and food that is purchased in small quantities costs far more.

It is now nearly four years since I started work, but still unemployment haunts me. It took at least three years to free ourselves from the debts that were the legacy of this period. In my life now, in order to progress, I have to obtain a place on a course, leave my employment and re-apply two years later at a higher grade. Few people understand the real fear that I feel in even thinking of taking this line of action, and it is highly unlikely I would do so. Within the probation service there is the view that it is unknown for somebody not to be offered a job following completing this course. The course is two years long and I am aware that the Government is capable of many things in that time period and I would not trust fate in that way.

Even more immediate feelings come from wives or parents. It is not an uncommon experience at my surgery for wives to sit nervously pummelling the side of the small wooden table which sits between me and my constituents. Invariably she will say that she knows there are no jobs, but couldn't I persuade an employer to give her husband just an interview. It would make such a difference to his morale. It would signal hope. He's decent. He's a good man. You see he's . . . But the sentence rarely gets finished. The eyes are already glassed over with tears.

How these husbands and wives must long, if not for a job, for a time when it no longer hurts, when the ache at the pit of the stomach is no longer noticeable. Who can blame people in this position for wanting to appear as though the curse which has been cast on them does not matter?

Parents come, too, about their children, many of whom have no chance whatsoever of finding a job, no matter how many training courses they attend. The situation is worse for those parents who are themselves unemployed. The benefits are so low and for parents to ask their children, who often have had so few material possessions, to pay a share in the rent is, in so many instances, the last straw. What is one supposed to say to parents who have done everything in their power to make a success of their children, who have taught them to live by the rules, who have practised what a loving family is about, and yet have to ask the children to leave so they, the parents, will have their meagre social security money increased? And what can be said to those parents who ask about job chances in a town where there are so few opportunities? There is no comfort in the fact that there are possibly a million other parents posing exactly the same question.

Naturalizing the Tragedy of Mass Unemployment

Why isn't unemployment the burning political issue which commands a major part of the Government's time and that of Parliament? What are the trade unions and employers up to? Why do we all go about pretending our business is more important than attending to this issue? Why has the political debate about those without work turned sour?

Part of the answer must lie with those politicians who, from the mid-1960s, let the situation deteriorate and unemployment levels rise. Once that started to happen there was rarely a point of such significant change that a new approach was demanded. One such point, however, did occur during the Heath Government when unemployment rose for the first time in the post-war world to over a million (the rise in 1947 was temporary), but the consequences of this had a boomerang effect on political debate since then. Some Government policies were reversed, culminating in the disastrous credit boom strategy carried out by the then Chancellor, Lord Barber. Politicians made much of this mismanagement as a reason for not attempting to pursue full employment policies again.

This was the position Mrs Thatcher inherited as her Government went about publicly confirming that a full employment policy could no longer be a prime political objective of governments. Full employment wasn't a realizable objective. This was the argument pushed by Mrs Thatcher with all the force and authority she could muster. Even to talk in such terms would lead to a cruel deception of those without work.

The debate about unemployment was successfully switched in the 1980s from a political programme which contained valuable proposals (like the numbers of people who should be in employment as an objective), to a programme which elevates inanimate objectives such as price stability. Even defence of this U-turn has itself changed. Originally, the proponents were careful to spell out that their new creed would lead directly to an expansion of the jobs market. Now the record has altered. Aiming for price stability *will help create* the conditions necessary to expand employment is the argument presented now by Government apologists. It seems a long time since human beings were the subject of government economic policy.

It cannot be said that this success in dethroning the full employment objective has been won in the face of great political opposition. There have, of course, been the ritual objections, but no alternative policies have been put forward by the Labour Party which is still feeling constrained by past Labour governments' inability to prevent unemployment from rising. Frank Dobson's recent statements on the importance of regaining full employment hopefully denote a change of tack. The failure to develop a coherent strategy is one of a number of intellectual failures in this whole wretched saga.

Another intellectual failure must also be confronted. Unemployment hardly appears on the agenda of economists. But what more important topic could there be? In a heartening exception to this general rule, Malcolm Sawyer, in an inaugural lecture at the University of Leeds, addressed this very aspect of the debate. With a light touch of irony he recalled how the irrelevance of economics to much of the real world can be found in Lionel (Lord) Robbins' classical definition of the subject. In 1932 Robbins was moved to write that economics was 'the science which studies human behaviour as a relationship between ends and scarce means which have alternative uses' and that, thereby, economic analysis 'focuses attention on a particular aspect of behaviour, the form imposed by the influence of scarcity'. As Joan Robinson pointed out at the time, 1932 was not the most appropriate time to assert this definition. The major economic problem of the time was not scarcity of resources, but a major scarcity of demand for those resources. Once again it seems economists are hell-bent on ignoring today's major economic problems by refusing even to include employment in many of their forecasts.

It is time to call a halt to this retreat and to make full employment a major subject of the political debate. As a first move Labour MPs need to express more effectively the despair and hopelessness of so many of their constituents. This righteous anger needs to be followed by the Party committing itself to working out how to achieve full employment which is a vital part of the national recovery programme advanced in the introduction to this book. At an institutional level we need to consider what part the EC and the government can and should play; what should be expected from employers and trade unions; what should be the role of our education system and what will be the responsibilities of each and every one of us, including the unemployed? Moreover, we shall need to consider how we exercize our power in wage bargaining once the economy starts to grow and create jobs.

The Four Barriers to Full Employment

It would be irresponsible to claim that the return to full employment merely requires an act of political will and courage. While these two qualities are necessary if full employment is to be regained there are a number of major institutional barricades impeding the way towards this objective. How we surmount these barricades is part of the intellectual task which confronts us. I will discuss briefly each of the main obstacles to give some idea of the amount of work which needs to be done if the rhetoric of full employment is going to be given some reality.

The first obstacle which we need to take note of is the

PSBR. According to the Government's own figures, PSBR is expected to rise to a staggering £50 billion in 1993–94. Even after the record tax increase in the 1993 budget the Chancellor still expects the PSBR to be around the £37 billion mark at the end of this parliament. No western government has ever run a budget deficit of this magnitude before, so it is impossible to say with any historical insight what the likely consequences will be. Given the economy's global nature, the Keynesian view that public investment does not necessarily squeeze out private investment is going to be given a quite unexpectedly vigorous testing over the next couple of years.

The other part of this Tory 'double whammy' concerns the balance of payments. Britain even when in deep recession turned in a £1 billion deficit each month on its trade account. In 1981 the balance of payments was in handsome surplus to the tune of £8 billion. It was possible then to advocate reflating the economy out of recession without being ambushed by a balance of payments crisis. Reflating with a balance of payments deficit is a very different matter. It is not impossible that, if we are forced to finance a growing trade deficit brought about by reflating the economy, the debt repayment may become larger than the resulting increase in national income.

The record PSBR and the current account deficit are now interacting and affecting the level at which the British economy can grow. The Treasury badly needs to increase the rate of growth in order to bring down the PSBR level. More people in work means higher tax revenues and lower social security expenditure, leaving a much-reduced PSBR. Economic growth, starting from the basis of a weak balance of trade, will, however, soon run up against an unsustainable trade gap. A three per cent growth rate is required to begin reducing the level of unemployment and the PSBR. However, given the effect of a mounting trade deficit, Bill Martin of the merchant bank UBS Phillips and Drew estimates that a further deterioration in the current account deficit will restrict growth to a mere one per cent. But the price of containing the current account deficit is a further deterioration in the already massive PSBR.

The second major obstacle is the structure of the deregulated financial services sector. Events over the past few years, following deregulation, highlight the changes which have occurred in the relationship between this sector and the country's manufacturing base. J. M. Keynes, who was a distinguished practitioner on the Stock Exchange as well as a gifted observer of what occurred there, wrote in 1936:

> The position is serious when enterprise becomes the bubble on the whirlpool of speculation. When the capital development of a country becomes a by-product of the activities of a casino, the job is likely to be ill-done. The measure of success obtained by Wall Street, regarded as an institution of which the proper social purpose is to train new investment into the most profitable channels in terms of future yield, cannot be claimed to be one of the outstanding triumphs of *laissez-faire* capitalism – which is not surprising, if I am right in thinking that the best brains of Wall Street have been in fact directed towards a different directive.

Anyone who watched the events of Black (or was it White?) Wednesday on television will have seen how the world has changed since Keynes wrote those words. It was not a case of enterprise being a bubble on the whirlpool of speculation, but of a country's entire economy being subjected to the mercies of the speculators. Stuart Holland estimates that ninety per cent of foreign exchange transactions are now currency speculation, as opposed to ten per cent at the time of exchange controls. Moreover, half of the money gained by foreign exchange deals came from speculating in European currencies. One lesson to draw from these events, which is developed later, is the need for concerted European action, not only in combating international currency speculation but in attempting to move back to full employment.

127

Malcolm Sawyers's view on this issue is important. At his inaugural lecture he concluded that a successfully productive economy capable of generating low levels of employment requires a financial sector which serves the needs of the productive sector, rather than the reverse.

This conclusion also needs to be considered when formulating a policy of moving the economy back to full employment. It ties in with the proposal in the last chapter that members of pension schemes should own their own pension funds. Due weight has already been given to the spread of private pension schemes. Not only have millions and millions of lives been transformed by the payments from occupational pensions, but the fear of ending one's days in dire poverty has been abolished for the majority of the population. Nothing can detract from this success. But the debate must move on. The urgent task now is to get the pensions industry to see that the next stage of its development must be to channel a greater proportion of pension savings directly into investment, rather than allowing them to be absorbed into the buying of securities (i.e., the ownership of existing capital stock). With an extraordinary amount of national savings now directed into pension funds this reform is important if the financing of British industry is to be put on an equal footing with its competitors. The pension reforms already advocated should lay down the basis for a more secure funding of British industry.

The third institutional barrier to full employment stems from the need to be able to ensure that the level of aggregate demand in the economy is adequate to meet the full employment target. This country's increasing propensity to import was mentioned earlier. In adjusting the level of aggregate demand this development must be taken into account. The weakening of our industrial base suggests that any counter-employment stimulus should come from an increase in investment aimed at improving the country's infrastructure, as this has little effect initially on the demand for imports. In the 1992 Autumn Statement the Government moved towards a capital programme stimulus, although even this modest concession to alleviate unemployment had to compete for funds with the growing costs of joblessness. Moreover, the Government did not claim that the measure was sufficient to stop unemployment rising. If creating jobs is really to be a priority, the Government must abandon its medieval accounting methods and bring forward medium term investment so that the haemorrhage of employees can be stemmed now.

Full Employment and Price Stability

The last but not by any means least significant of the obstacles in the way of achieving and then sustaining full employment is the extent to which inflationary pressures are exacerbated in the economy as it is expanded, and particularly as the economy approaches full employment. On this front Labour will need to drop its traditional silence and speak out for countering wage-push inflation which is fundamental if full employment, once achieved, is to be sustained. Moreover, a full employment policy which does not seek to deal with these inflationary pressures will have almost no appeal for the electorate.

In some ways this obstacle will be more difficult to surmount than the others which have been mentioned. For the plain truth is that we simply do not yet know how we can successfully contain wage-push pressures as the economy moves towards full employment. But dealing with wage-push inflation has potentially become more not less difficult since the collapse of full employment. The move to plant bargaining of the 1960s and 1970s, together with the recent government initiatives to decentralize civil service pay, adds to wage-push pressures in the economy as it begins to grow again.

We, therefore, need to ask why it is that employees feel that the only opportunity they have to defend their interests is through pay demands. In the previous chapter I advocated the enfranchisement of pension funds so that individuals have the right to own the considerable share of capital that they and their employers have built up within the firm's pension scheme. I believe that, to some extent, this fundamental change in the ownership of British industry could itself lead to a change in attitudes which will be conducive to running the economy at a high level of employment without prices rising rapidly. Wage and salary demands will not be pitched at some unseen *rentier* class, for the worker himself will know exactly what his own *rentier* class status is.

Defeating Mass Unemployment for the Second Time

Given the extent of these institutional barriers, no one can be under any illusion that the move back to full employment will be easily accomplished. The magnitude of the task becomes even more apparent if a comparison is made between the size of today's problem and that after the great crash in 1929. In a recent report Robert Skidelsky and Liam Halligan listed the economic differences between today's slump and that of sixty years ago. Their main conclusions are

• The British slump over the last two years has been of the same magnitude as that of the 1929–31 period.

• Then, output in the US and the rest of Europe fell by 29 per cent compared with only 6–7 per cent in Great Britain. This time the reverse is true. Britain has suffered the largest fall in national income.

• Unemployment then was much more concentrated in the declining industries and regions. This time it is more evenly spread thereby opening up the possibility of an even recovery.

• There are major differences in the movement of prices. Then prices fell by 12 per cent. During 1990–92 prices merely ceased to rise as quickly: down from a 9.4 per cent to a 3.4 per cent increase a year.

The picture is not therefore one of total gloom. Our export markets, on the continent and in the USA, are in very much better shape this time round than they were during the 1929–31 Depression. But the difference in what is happening to prices now compared with then underlines the difficulties in achieving full employment. Reflation, ignoring for the moment the constraints from the current PSBR or the balance of the trade deficit, is an option with less of a down side when prices are actually falling, than when there is already inflation within the economy.

There is, however, one other major difference between today's recession and the 1929 crash which tells us much about the point at which today's debate begins. Then, unlike now, as Robert Skidelsky reminds us in his classic *Politicians and the Slump,*

> an important section of influential opinion had ... come around to the view that traditional remedies would not meet the new economic facts; thus by 1929 there had developed a rigorous debate on economic questions.

One reason why that vigorous debate was having an impact by 1929 was the political initiative Lloyd George took in 1925 in establishing the Liberal Industrial Inquiry. Three years later what became known as the first Yellow Book was published entitled *Britain's Industrial Future*. This report examined the measures which needed to be taken if Britain was to re-establish itself successfully in those export markets which had been lost during the war.

Policies designed to this end would have had an obvious effect on unemployment levels. During 1929, the election year, academics supporting the Liberal Party addressed the specific measures which could be taken to deal with what Pigou had termed 'the intractable million' (those who were condemned to permanent unemployment). Two carefully reasoned reports were published. The first came from Lloyd George, Lord Lothian and Seebohm Rowntree and

was published under the explicit title *We Can Conquer Unemployment*. This was followed by a similar effort in which J. M. Keynes and Hubert Henderson asked *Can Lloyd George Do It?* The answer was a resounding 'Yes'.

Robert Skidelsky evaluates the political impact of these initiatives:

> It was a supreme attempt by the Liberal leader to wrest the initiative from his political opponents and never was such an effort sustained by a more impressive array of publications and policies – intellectually the most distinguished that had ever been placed before the British electorate.

Labour should now take a similar major political initiative. The Commission on Social Justice's terms of reference limit it to analysing public policies, particularly in the fields of employment, taxation and social welfare, which means that it will not have time to devote its talents exclusively to the level of employment, much of its energy being spent on debating how to divide the existing national income more fairly. Labour should be seen as the party of economic opportunity and should establish a parallel commission with this aim. A Commission for Economic Opportunity should begin the task of working out policies necessary for re-establishing full employment. Each of the obstacles, or barricades, needs to be countered in a detailed and reasoned manner.

A Commission for Economic Opportunity should view the creation of full employment as an issue which must be tackled at an EC level. Instead of trying to persuade the country of the wisdom of Maastricht, would not a more constructive approach be to debate what institutional moves are necessary within the EC to meet clearly defined employment level objectives? The Maastricht Treaty, and following treaties, would, therefore, be based on Europe needing to adapt its institutions to meet real objectives, rather than to fit in with an abstract theory about European union.

Action is also needed within the machinery of British government and Labour must show how it would develop a strategy to tackle this once it is elected. It is instructive to look at how the Labour and national governments initiated a new machinery in Whitehall which attempted to meet the size of the unemployment challenge those governments faced.

During the 1929 election campaign MacDonald promised that if Labour won it would set up a 'brain' to deal with unemployment, which in structure and function would resemble the Committee of Imperial Defence. MacDonald seemed to envisage a Ministry of Employment headed by himself, rather as Churchill headed the Ministry of Defence whilst he was Prime Minister. Sadly the new Ministry failed to materialize. Special responsibility for unemployment was given to the Lord Privy Seal, J. H. Thomas, whose friends would hardly have described him as a brain, whatever else they might have said of him.

MacDonald was, however, more successful at adding to, rather than restructuring, the machinery of government. Again, there are important lessons for today. By the summer of 1930 the Government had two 'brains' within the Whitehall machine. The first was the Economic Advisory Committee; the second, Sir John Anderson's Committee of Civil Servants.

Sir John Anderson's Committee of Civil Servants, after taking six weeks to review the debate, advised the Prime Minister that little could be done. Indeed, civil servants then spent a great deal of their time writing papers to Ministers arguing that failure would be the inevitable result of any changes in policy. While this would predictably be the Treasury's reaction today, the response of economists was very different. In the unprecedented situation of persistent long-term unemployment Robert Skidelsky notes that most of the senior economists of the 1930s were prepared to rethink their positions in an attempt to devise policy proposals which were relevant to lessening unemployment. This reaction contrasted starkly with that of the civil service group.

The response of the economic establishment in the 1930s and today's equivalent group could not be more different. Senior economists, generally speaking, have failed to address themselves at all to the question of why there is such persistent long-term unemployment, and at such a high level, and of what can be done to combat this situation. Even the wise critics from the City and academia who the Treasury has appointed will offer little hope of new thinking unless they are able to redefine the economic agenda, treating unemployment as the most pressing problem they face, rather than as an epiphenomenon of price stability. Here a lesson can be learned from the United States whose Council for Economic Advisors, which was itself formed by the 1946 Full Employment Act, managed, against the odds, to maintain employment as a national issue even during the Reagan years.

What immediate actions are called for? First the Economic Advisory Committee should be re-established with an initial task of challenging the economic profession on this very point. It should, for example, begin a dialogue with the Economic and Social Research Council to ask why it is that so little of a substantial economic research budget is directed to those wishing to provide answers to today's most pressing economic problem.

More immediately, the Economic Advisory Committee could initiate a public debate on what policies a government can pursue in furtherance of a full employment objective. I end by suggesting how a comprehensive full employment strategy can be developed.

The natural starting point is the golden age of full employment with which we were blessed after World War Two. How can that success be explained? Was it an exceptionally lucky fluke or are there causes that can be re-created?

A number of factors accounted for that post-war success, one of which was the Marshall Plan. Finance from that programme ensured that western Europe could get back to work and that it would have the money to buy the goods and services which its inhabitants both needed and could produce. With most of eastern Europe and the former Soviet Union having the greatest of difficulties in making a successful transfer from a state to a free market, a similar Group of Seven initiative is required today. Such a policy is as morally important as it is economically sound. It would help revive eastern Europe, and what was the USSR, and so provide new and expanding export markets for our goods.

Second, the strategic position of the German economy must be recognized and acted upon despite the phobia we have about it in Britain. There is a reluctance to accept the role which Germany now plays in western Europe, and indeed, on the world stage. I leave aside its emerging political role. Economically, it is Europe's dominant economy. What happens to the German economy, therefore, has a major impact on all EC economies, as well as those of the surrounding territories.

Not surprisingly, what was the West German government made a hash of its economic reunion programme. The task, after all, has never been attempted before. Germany is currently borrowing on the world market to finance its reunion programme. With a cost which is of comparable size to our social security budget, the surprise is not that German interest rates are so high, but that they are so relatively low. German interest rates will not be reduced substantially until this reunion programme has been successfully completed. Another move the German Government should therefore consider is how, and to what extent, can the EC help financially in the investment programme in what was East Germany. The quicker this programme is accomplished, the quicker German interest rates will fall; given the influence of the German economy on all European states, the quicker, therefore, will be the resumption of a higher rate of growth within the EC.

The third proposal looks to Europe. For those wishing to promote the cause of Europe in terms of economic union, dealing with unemployment offers a major opportunity. That aim should be the starting block for all discussions of how well EC institutions service Europe, as well as looking at what economic and organizational reforms are necessary. Common European interests need to be emphasized along the following lines. Once a package of EC financial help for what was East Germany has been agreed — organized perhaps through increased borrowing powers for the private sector of the European Investment Bank — the British government should attempt to get agreement to co-ordinate a lowering of interest rates throughout Europe.

In an attempt to increase trade amongst member nations Britain should propose a cut in VAT to operate uniformly throughout the EC for all those economies where GDP is falling. The government should also propose that any additional increase in public expenditure, now aimed at creating jobs, should be exempt from the 3 per cent overall budget deficit conditions which are part of the Maastricht Treaty. Lastly, the government should mobilize the antagonism against currency speculators which is now European-wide. A common tax on currency speculation is long overdue.

The last suggestion relates directly to two actions upon which the British government can immediately embark. The first is concerned with eliminating the fiscal discrimination against the creation of full-time jobs. To ensure that the spread of part-time jobs is not the only option for employers expanding the job base, the structure of national insurance contributions should be overhauled. Currently, there are no contributions from employers or employees if the latter earn less than £56 per week.

National insurance contributions now operate as a tax on the creation of full-time jobs. Over the 1980s the numbers in employment expanded by a million and was accounted for almost exclusively by an increase in part-time workers. From September 1981 until December 1989 the increase in the numbers in work rose by 1,077,000. Of these, 1,035,000 were part-time workers. Whilst some people wish to work part-time, the cry of many of my constituents is that all that is offered is part-time, often very badly paid, work. They take these opportunities, but what they want is a full-time job with a full-time wage packet.

As outlined in Chapter Four, employers' contributions should become payable on the first one pound of a worker's earnings. As the aim would not be to raise additional revenue (and thereby tax job creation in a general way), the move should be revenue neutral. Contributions for other workers would fall. The overall rate of employers' contribution to the National Insurance Fund would not rise.

The other main initiative immediately open to the government is to challenge the cartel the employed have organized against the unemployed. Many will be appalled, or even angered, by the suggestion that they have ganged up against the unemployed, but that is how it looks to those in the dole queue. The ganging up process is operated through the wage and salary bargaining machinery.

There is talk that German trade unions are beginning to challenge this cartel arrangement. Their idea is to offer to freeze wage and salary settlements, provided that any productivity increase is set aside to create new jobs. This is one challenge on which those inside the employment cartel should pick up. The consequences would have to be spelt out. It would be a salary and wage standstill for most workers. That, with current inflation, would mean a cut of 3 per cent or so in living standards each year. Is this a price workers would pay to offer a hand up to those in the dole queue? I believe it is. There would have to be careful discussions as well to ensure that the productivity gains were used to create new jobs. But that would not be impossible.

A greater challenge would be to begin discussing with the employment cartel what their attitude would be to a fully fledged work sharing proposal. The aim here would be to set out what would be involved now if full employment was to be achieved by a worksharing approach. A single example illustrates the size of the redistribution which such an approach entails. If every member of the employment cartel were prepared to accept a 12.5 per cent cut in hours worked and wages or salaries drawn and if the released resources went to creating jobs for those who are unemployed, Britain could return to full employment in a relatively short space of time. The buck, of course, stops with each of us in the employment cartel. Are we prepared to see our living standards reduced (and the hours that we work simultaneously cut) to welcome aboard the unemployed? I am not suggesting that such a policy is the only way to achieve full employment, but it is one that should be placed firmly on the political agenda. If it does nothing more it demonstrates that the debate about full employment is, like all great political issues, about power. With power goes command over resources. Proposing the simplest way back to full employment, whilst stating the very real cost to those already in employment, will begin to shift the political argument.

This then needs to be followed up by a further challenge to the employment cartel. Of all groups of claimants the worst treated are the jobless, and yet these are the very people who have been conscripted into Britain's unemployment army to wage war on inflation. The last proposal that I make here is for an unemployment tax which would be levied through the National Insurance scheme on all of us in employment. The sums raised would be used to finance more adequate benefits for those unemployed. This proposal would have two immediate advantages.

The first is that it would raise the living standards of the unemployed, in particular those who have been out of the labour market longest as the benefits could be directed particularly towards them. The cost of unemployment would be shared more fairly. But the bill of helping the unemployed would be significant. The tax would be clearly designated on everybody's wage or salary slip so that each member of the employment cartel would be more aware of the cost of government inactivity in the face of mass unemployment. This unemployment tax should be large enough not merely to raise the level of unemployment pay, but to cover contributions to the pension funds of those whose unemployment is seen as a necessary bulwark against inflation.

The disappearance of pounds from the pockets of those in the employment cartel will help to concentrate the electorate's mind on the need for the government to initiate a policy of moving the economy back to full employment. Not to do so would mean a financial penalty on the very people who could demand action by the government.

Conclusion

Most of us in the western world have experienced living in an age of full employment. The goal of full employment is not, therefore, a foolish illusion peddled by a few left-wing cranks. It is a political objective which has been achieved and which could be achieved once again, even though that is not the view of the majority of politicians. Achieving a goal of full employment is urgent in human terms. It is also important to be conscious of the restraints within which the British government operates. While there are tasks which the government can immediately carry out to help expand the employment base in this country, any sensible full employment policy must be implemented in unison with our European partners. Europe must prepare for the great transformation of economic power which is currently underway and which is tilting economic advantage clearly in favour of the newly emerging Asian economic superpowers.

The Vision Thing Again

For most of this century British politics have been governed by a ruling consensus. The prevailing consensus of the inter-war years was dominated by Baldwin and MacDonald whose concern was to prevent anything out of the ordinary happening. It was an age of lost opportunities and stunted lives. This ruling consensus was swept away by the ideas which took root in the public's imagination during the war years. With Britain first surviving and then conquering the Nazi menace, the inter-war consensus of muddling through lost out as organized efficiency was seen to work, first on the home front and then on the second front which was opened up in Europe.

The post-war welfare state consensus lasted well over a quarter of a century, and indeed still has much appeal. But the ration book mentality of the Left – the Crippsian delight in denying choice not only to the working class but to many middle-class families as well – was being challenged long before the slow slide from full employment. The open challenge to the remains of that post-war consensus came from the Thatcher Governments, spurred on by three consecutive election victories. For all Mrs Thatcher's personal achievements no new consensus has been established. How could it when the thrust of her ideas was about the superiority of untrammelled market forces? These selfsame forces are the ones which have wrought havoc with so much of British industry and have left the economy in a wounded state.

One reason why British politics is so lifeless is that no new consensus has emerged to give drive and vision, purpose and hope to voters and politicians alike. Voters condemn politicians for failing to come up with 'the big idea'. Yet politicians have rarely played this innovative role. No one, for example, went into World War Two thinking that Britain was about to embark upon another of her silent revolutions. Events gave rise to 'the big idea'. Events again are forging 'the big idea'. In a world which has lost its sense of deference, only danger awaits a political community which believes it can permanently sideline into unemployment one in six of its population of working age.

The consensus this time needs to set itself on a wider stage. Economic forces are working ever more surely on a world scale, and Britain, with her relatively tiny resources, cannot buck the world trend, if Mrs Thatcher will forgive the phrase. What is required is the skill to maximize our advantages and a resourcefulness to negotiate alliances which promote this country's interest. Those alliances which play out on a world stage – such as GATT – and more regional groupings – as in the European community – are the framework within which Britain's future is governed.

The idea that is central to this book – regaining full employment – straddles both the global and domestic stage. The successful conclusion of the GATT Uruguay Round is essential for Britain's economic well-being. Mobilizing the EC can have a clearer impact on employment policies, but the British government has its own role to play both in stirring up the EC to meet this objective and in maximizing the opportunities it has on the home front.

It is at this point that the welfare reforms argued for in this book play their part, not merely as objectives in their own right, but as part of a new consensus built around full employment. The aim is to cut the welfare budget, not by penalizing the poor, but by locking an increasing number of people into the benefits of income from work and wealth. This requires two revolutions. First, the deliberate construction of exits from welfare dependency, so that the maximum number of individuals and families can harness the opportunities offered to them by exercizing their own self-interest.

Second, the economy must move back to full employment so that individuals' self-help and effort can be adequately rewarded. If history is any guide, the speed by which the new consensus could be established will surprise only politicians.

The moral framework to buttress a new consensus is there. Indeed it was present throughout the Thatcher era. Its problem was that it was unable to find any effective political expression. The widespread sharing of certain values was reported in all gallup polls carried out on voters' preferences. Poll after poll recorded the voters' support for what were generally regarded as Left policies – higher spending on the health service, on education and on pensions. This same group was responsible for a record four consecutive Tory election wins. Some commentators have attempted to explain away this apparent inconsistency by arguing that voters were either dishonest, or that they wished to appear respectable and give what they thought would be the acceptable answers. A more obvious explanation is that the answers on priorities gave a totally accurate view of the voters' preferences. The Conservatives won, despite their failure to reflect the country's overall priorities, because voters regarded Labour in the 1980s and early 1990s as unelectable.

For Labour to do better next time, and even win, it has to be seen as being serious about running the economy. The 'old lags' game of just opposing the government and nothing more might have worked in the 1950s and 1960s. With four massive electoral defeats in a row it simply won't wash with the electorate this time. Labour has positively to win over voters by showing how it will handle the economy. That means the Party has to lead the debate on how, for example, it would react to today's £50 billion public sector borrowing requirement if it were in government. What action would the Party take to prevent an additional £35 billion from being added to the PSBR (which will happen at the time of the next election unless the borrowing requirement is changed) to service the public sector debt? By answering this question Labour will begin to take over the economic debate and will cease simply to adapt itself to whatever policy stance the Government is forced to adopt.

Dealing with the PSBR is an immediate issue. So too is the more fundamental question of restoring full employment, the consequences of which straddle both global and domestic stages. Action such as establishing a cabinet committee for economic opportunities is not open to a party in opposition. But the leading opposition party could begin by establishing such a committee to begin the long overdue debate on how best to extend job opportunities in Britain on its own or more sensibly in alliance with the Liberal Democrats. The issue of how such a strategy can be shared by other European Community countries must also be part of the agenda.

Striking out in these ways will simultaneously achieve two crucial political breakthroughs. It will capture the frontier of the political debate, with politicians again calling upon the advice of economists, industrialists, trade unionists and others on how best to tackle the most important issue facing the country. The search for a viable economic policy would itself be the mechanism whereby the clear moral preferences of voters, which have influenced radical politics for the whole of this century and which are still recorded in every opinion poll finding, could again be found effective in the ballot boxes of the next election.

SOURCES

CHAPTER ONE

The best overall study of the 1992 election is David Butler and Dennis Cavanagh's *The 1992 General Election* (Oxford, 1993). Butler joined forces with Donald Stokes to produce *Political Change in Britain* (Macmillan, 1969). The most pertinent of Ivor Crewe's many studies is 'The decline of labour and the decline of Labour', *Papers in Politics and Government*, No. 65, 1989. The work of Anthony Heath, Roger Jowell and John Curtis referred to in this chapter is *How Britain Votes* (Pergamon, 1983). James Alt's work referred to in the text is *The Politics of Economic Decline* (CUP, 1979). J. K. Galbraith's *Culture of Contentment* was published by Sinclair-Stevenson in 1992. The lecture I gave in 1976 on selling council houses was published as *Do we need Council Houses* by the Catholic Housing Aid Society in the same year. Jack Straw has written about the shortcomings of the Labour Party's constitution. See his pamphlet 'Policy and ideology', Blackburn Labour Party, 36 Wellington Street, Blackburn, BB1 8AF. Will Marshall and Martin Schram edited *Mandate for Change*, which gives the background for the policy formation for the Clinton election campaign.

CHAPTER TWO

The most informed and witty analysis of Mrs Thatcher's stewardship of the economy is to be found in Ian Gilmour's *Dancing with Dogma* (Simon & Schuster, 1992). For more detailed information on changes to the labour market as it affects poorer paid workers the publications of the Low Pay Unit are crucial source material. The Low Pay Unit's address is 27 Amwell Street, London, EC1R 1UN. Jan Penn's book on income distribution was published under the title *Income Distribution* (Pelican, 1974). The Unemployment Unit is an important source of information on how best to interpret the unemployment data. Its address is 409 Brixton Road, London, SW9 7DG. The publications by the House of Commons Social Security Select Committee on the numbers on low income are to be found in *Low Income Statistics*, HC 376, 1990, which disproved the working of the trickle-down theory which was claimed by Mrs Thatcher, and *Low Income Statistics*, HC 359, 1992. The most up-to-date presentation of the Government's stance is to be found in *Households Below Average Income: A statistical analysis 1979 – 1988/ 89*, HMSO, 1992. Also worth consulting is the Institute of Fiscal Study's *Poverty Statistics: A guide for the perplexed*, written by Christopher Giles and Stephen Webb which was published in 1993.

CHAPTER THREE
Gunnar Myrdal's work quoted in the text is *Challenge to Affluence* (Victor Gollancz, 1963) and his definition of the underclass is to be found on page 23. A good survey of the American debate about the underclass can be found in Christopher Jencks and Paul Peterson (eds.), *The Urban Underclass* (Brookings Institute, 1991). The references to, and quotations from, the three bench-mark studies of babies born in a single week during 1946, 1958 and 1970 are summarized in Frank Field's *Losing Out: the emergence of Britain's underclass* (Basil Blackwell, 1989). The reader will also find quoted in this volume the studies which have attempted to gauge the changing social structure of Britain which are referred to in this chapter. The survey by Barnardos and Youth Aid on the plight of the young single homeless was published in 1993. Called *Four Year's Severe Hardship*, the report was written by Ianthe Maclogan.

CHAPTER FOUR
The income of pensioner households comes from a parliamentary answer which was given in *Hansard*, 12 February 1993 col. 840 written. The information on the numbers of lone parents, and the benefits they claim, was provided by the House of Commons Library. One of the most interesting projects run by young single mothers goes under the title of the Barton Hill Project. The address of this group is c/o Community Leisure Office, Russell Town Avenue, Bristol, BS5 9LT.

CHAPTER FIVE
The Social Security Select Committee published a background on pension developments in this country in their report on the Maxwell theft of pension funds. *The Operation of Pension Funds* was published as a House of Commons paper in March 1992 (61–ii). A summary of the pensions debate is to be found in Matthew Owen and Frank Field's Fabian pamphlet entitled *Making Sense of Pensions* (557) which was published in 1993. Philip Chappel wrote three pioneering studies on the reform of pensions and this chapter reflects his views and those of Lord Vinson. The first two were written with Lord Vinson. *Personal and portable pensions for all* was published in 1983 and *Owners all: a proposal for personal investment* in 1985. *Pensioners and Privilege*

came out in 1988. All three publications were published by the Centre for Policy Studies.

CHAPTER SIX

Malcolm Sawyer's Inaugural Lecture was given in Leeds in 1992 under the title of *Unemployment and the dismal science*. Keynes's best known classic is *Employment Income and Money*. The review cited of this current slump with the 1930s comes from Robert Skidelsky's and Liam Halligan's Social Market Foundation publication, *Another Great Depression? Historical Lessons for the 1990s*, Report No. 2, SMF, 1992. Robert Skidelsky's classic, *Politicians and the Slump* was published by Penguin Books in 1967. The two references to this book appear on pages 16 and 67 respectively. The major study on the Economic Advisory Committee was published under that name by OUP in 1977. It was written by Susan Howson and Donald Winch. One of the most provocative writers on the question of full employment is Sam Brittain and his column can be regularly seen in the *Financial Times*. For an equally important contribution to the debate readers should consult the publications of the Employment Policy Institute. Their address is Southbank House, Black Prince Road, London, SE1 7SJ. Bryan Gould heads a Labour Party Full Employment Group whose director is Bob Harrison. The address is 4 Armand Way, Watford, Herts, WD1 3SQ.

INDEX

Index

The Unprincipled Society
New Demands and Old Politics

David Marquand

'The most coherent and simulating book of political analysis I have read in the 1980s.' Hugo Young

'Of all the many hundreds of books spawned by the search for the causes of Britain's economic decline, none that I have read has ranged so widely, probed so intelligently, or made more unanswerable sense. *The Unprincipled Society* could become the seminal work for the 1990s as Tony Crosland's *The Future of Socialism* was for the 1950s.' John Campbell, *The Times*

'Thank heavens for Professor David Marquand. *The Unprincipled Society* is original, lucid and elegantly written; it should be ordered in bulk. David Marquand has something new to say.'
Robert Harris, *Observer*

'This is one of the most profound and original analyses of Britain's relative economic decline – and of the intellectual and political forces underlying it – to have appeared in the last forty years. If British politicians, officials, businessmen and union leaders read only one book this year, it probably ought to be David Marquand's.' *Economist*

'In its breadth of vision and the quality of its argument this book stands far above almost all else in the mode. It is an important and challenging work.' Stephen Howe, *New Statesman*

ISBN 0 00 686153 9

Fontana Press

Whitehall

Peter Hennessy

'The thinking man's *Yes Minister*.'

Lord Hunt, ex-secretary of the Cabinet

'Mr Hennessy has at last produced his magnum opus – more than 800 pages chronicling the history of Whitehall from the Norman Conquest to Norman Strauss. Along the way we also get an analysis of present-day ministries, a reform tract and a succession of the Great and Good . . . It is the best account of the British Civil Service ever produced. More than that, it is also, to use Edward Bridges' favourite word, enormous fun.'

Robert Harris, *Observer*

'The most thorough examination of the civil service and her ways yet published. It is ambitious in intent, sweeping in scope, meticulous in detail and penetrating in analysis. His judgements are fair, and sure to disappoint the ideologies of both left and right. Whitehall looks set to beome the standard work on the ways and byways of a hugely important and underexposed part of national life.'

Jeremy Paxman, *Independent*

'This is an outstanding book by a political historian and journalist who has himself become something of a national institution . . . Present and future ministers, whether seeking to alter the machine or merely to comprehend its puzzling idiom and culture, are certain to regard Hennessy's brilliant investigation as the indispensable guide.'

Ben Pimlott, *Sunday Times*

'*Whitehall* is much the best book on the British civil service ever to appear. Everyone who claims the slightest acquaintance with British government will have to read the book, indeed own it.'

Anthony King, *Economist*

ISBN 0 00 686180 6

Fontana Press

Demanding the Impossible

A History of Anarchism

Peter Marshall

'To be governed means that at every move, operation or transaction one is noted, registered, entered in a census, taxed, stamped, priced, assessed, patented, licensed, authorized, recommended, admonished, reformed . . . exploited, monopolized, extorted, pressured, mystified, robbed; all in the name of public utility and the general good.'

So said Proudhon in 1851, and from the Ancient Chinese to today's rebel youth many have agreed – among their number Godwin and Kropotkin, Bakunin and Malatesta, Tolstoy and Gandhi, the Ranters and the Situationists, de Sade and Thoreau, Wilde and Chomsky, anarcho-syndicalists and anarcha-feminists. Peter Marshall, in his inclusive, inspirational survey, gives back to the anarchistic, undiluted and undistorted, their secret history.

'Reading about anarchism is stimulating and funny and sad. What more can you ask of a book?'   Isabel Colegate, *The Times*

'Massive, scholarly, genuinely internationalist and highly enjoyable . . . this is the book Johnny Rotten ought to have read.'
David Widgery, *Observer*

'Large, labyrinthine, tentative: for me these are all adjectives of praise when applied to works of history, and *Demanding the Impossible* meets all of them. I now have a book – Marshall's solid 700 pages and more – to which I can direct readers when they ask me how soon I intend to bring my *Anarchism* up to date.'   George Woodcock, *Independent*

'This is the most comprehensive account of anarchist thought ever written. Marshall's knowledge is formidable and his enthusiasm engaging . . . he organizes a mass of diverse material with great subtlety and skill, presenting a good-tempered critique of each position with straightforward lucidity.'   J. B. Pick, *Scotsman*

ISBN 0 00 686245 4

Fontana Press

The Anatomy of Thatcherism

Shirley Robin Letwin

The Anatomy of Thatcherism explains why, for the first time in British history, a prime minister's name has become synonymous with an idea and a political movement. Dr Letwin argues that Thatcherism has prompted a fundamental re-alignment in British politics by focusing on a moral agenda rather than on an economic doctrine or a political theory. She introduces a new term – 'the vigorous virtues' – to describe what Thatcherites have aimed to cultivate in individual Britons and in the country as a whole.

The Anatomy of Thatcherism is a bold and searching book about how Britain changed between 1979 and 1991. It challenges truisms about British politics, and is indispensable reading both for those who believe in the future relevance of Thatcherism and for those who want to demolish it. And it will be of particular interest to those concerned with the history of British politics, as it shows how Thatcherism arose out of, and confronted, trends that permeated Toryism for the entire twentieth century.

Fontana

The Crooked Timber of Humanity

Chapters in the History of Ideas

Isaiah Berlin

'Reading Isaiah Berlin is always exhilarating.'

Anthony Storr, *Independent on Sunday*

'Berlin's preoccupations are constant. His commitment is to individual and collective liberty and to moral and political pluralism. His writing is an extended exploration of the conditions in which those ideals blossom and flourish or wither and perish. The eight essays collected here are all concerned with manifestations of anti-rationalism: utopianism, fascism, romanticism and nationalism are all passed in magisterial review. To read them is to sit at an unlit window and see the landscape of European thought illuminated by a spectacular display of fireworks.'

Ian McIntyre, *Independent*

'To read Isaiah Berlin is above all to listen to a voice, effervescent, quizzical, often self-mocking, but always full of gaiety and amusement. These essays remind the reader on every page of the many thousands of listeners over the decades for whom that voice has brought the drama and passion and imaginative depth of the intellectual tradition to which they belong unforgettably alive.'

John Dunn, *Times Literary Supplement*

ISBN 0 00 686221 7

Fontana Press

HarperCollins Paperbacks – Non-Fiction

HarperCollins is a leading publisher of paperback non-fiction. Below are some recent titles.

- ☐ STORM COMMAND Peter De La Billiere £5.99
- ☐ THE NEW EMPERORS Harrison Salisbury £8.99
- ☐ HAROLD WILSON Ben Pimlott £9.99
- ☐ AN AGENDA FOR BRITAIN Frank Field £6.99
- ☐ JUDY GARLAND David Shipman £6.99
- ☐ MARLENE DIETRICH Stephen Bach £7.99
- ☐ THE HONOURABLE COMPANY John Keay £8.99
- ☐ BRAVER MEN WALK AWAY Peter Gurney £5.99
- ☐ THIS IS ORSON WELLES Ed. Peter Bogdanovich £6.99

You can buy HarperCollins Paperbacks at your local bookshops or newsagents. Or you can order them from HarperCollins Paperbacks, Cash Sales Department, Box 29, Douglas, Isle of Man. Please send a cheque, postal or money order (not currency) worth the price plus 24p per book for postage (maximum postage required is £3.00 for orders within the UK).

NAME (Block letters)_____

ADDRESS_____

_____